AF479779

Andrei Cristian Pascu

BoK: Book Of Knowledge

Bucharest
2024

Title: BoK: Book Of Knowledge
Author: Andrei Cristian Pascu
Editor: Andrei Cristian Pascu
Publisher: Andrei Cristian Pascu
ISBN Number: 978-973-0-41015-0

Table of Contents

About This Book

The Author

Hello there, my name is Andrei!: I was born and raised in Romania. My goal with this book is to provide tools to conclude, or attempt to conclude, the existential questions that are howling inside some of us.

Education: Bachelor's Degree @ The University Of Sports & Performance (Europe, Romania, Bucharest).

Job & Career: Senior Web Developer / Software Engineer.

Big Five Personality: We'll discuss these in the book. My agreeableness and extraversion are average, but they can shift. My conscientiousness fluctuates from high to low based on interest. I am higher than average for males on the neuroticism front. I am hyper-open-minded for both subsets of this trait. More on this in "Map On: The Big Five."

Brain Configuration: In a measurable sense on the autistic front, in the form of Asperger's, which means here that I score at about 50/100 for various tests.
- I have a significant interest in things and a tendency toward seeing patterns.
- I have a low innate understanding of human beings, so I've developed all these systems. People are people, but I see these inner mechanisms as things, so I was interested in systems like these.
- This high interest in things and the tendency to see patterns worked well for me in the direction of a programmer's career.

Meaningful Events: When I was in my early teens, I was in a cult. It was not the worst cult, but still a cult; the main character thought of himself as the reincarnation of Jesus. I had a baby with a woman twice my age. I stayed with her and the baby for a short while, and then I left. After a few years, she left the country. I stayed in touch with her but couldn't be present in the kid's life, as I've become an adult. This situation created… inner issues, to call them mildly. What occurred inside was a traumatic reaction to those events. We will discuss what this means also. I've beaten my head against the wall, trying to fix it so I wouldn't randomly suffer anymore. I've fixed it, and I am in touch with my son. The trauma resolution chapter is my exact process; every step will be thoroughly explained.

The Book

Its Purpose: Every positive conclusion I ever arrived at is derived from these thinking tools. If you engulf yourself in this writing, your precise findings will differ, but the fundamental tools used will be the same as the ones I used.

Style Of Writing: In a word, it would be the brutalist style. You'll find the writing concise because, while this is technically a book, it serves as a thinking tool. Concrete examples will be provided, but only when absolutely necessary. The goal is to integrate these tools into our own lives and experiences. Too many examples might distract us, leading to the belief that the tool doesn't apply to our situation.

Ease Of Use: The English, for the most part, is kept simple; not everybody reading this is a native English speaker. I don't want you to check the dictionary or search online every 5-10 minutes. We want to be focused on the concepts at hand.

Relatability: Although this book is quite technical at times, I wish it was more relatable and comfortable when it could. You will find "we" quite a lot, so it's clear that you are not alone in this, not while reading this book, not ever.

Disclaimers

Anti-Trauma Work: After a significant event, it is best to let it rest for at least 18 months before starting the methods presented for trauma resolution. These 18 months are from scientific psychological work, which is not my guess. Jumping in too early may do more harm than good.

Scientific: All these are observations. There will be structures, such as the Dark Tetrad or The Big Five, that were tested rigorously by psychologists. I observed parts that map well between themselves and other systems of perceiving the inner world.

Religious: We will tackle mostly high-level concepts and attempt to map and overlap them with other structures. This will not be an in-depth analysis, although stories, ideas, and virtues that stem from religions can be analyzed and integrated through these maps and systems.

Hierarchy Of: The Meaning Of Life

Hierarchy, Structure & Movement

We will start with the highest-level view possible. After establishing this initial framework, we will move to the next chapter, The Tower, to get a clear view of the details of the inner world.

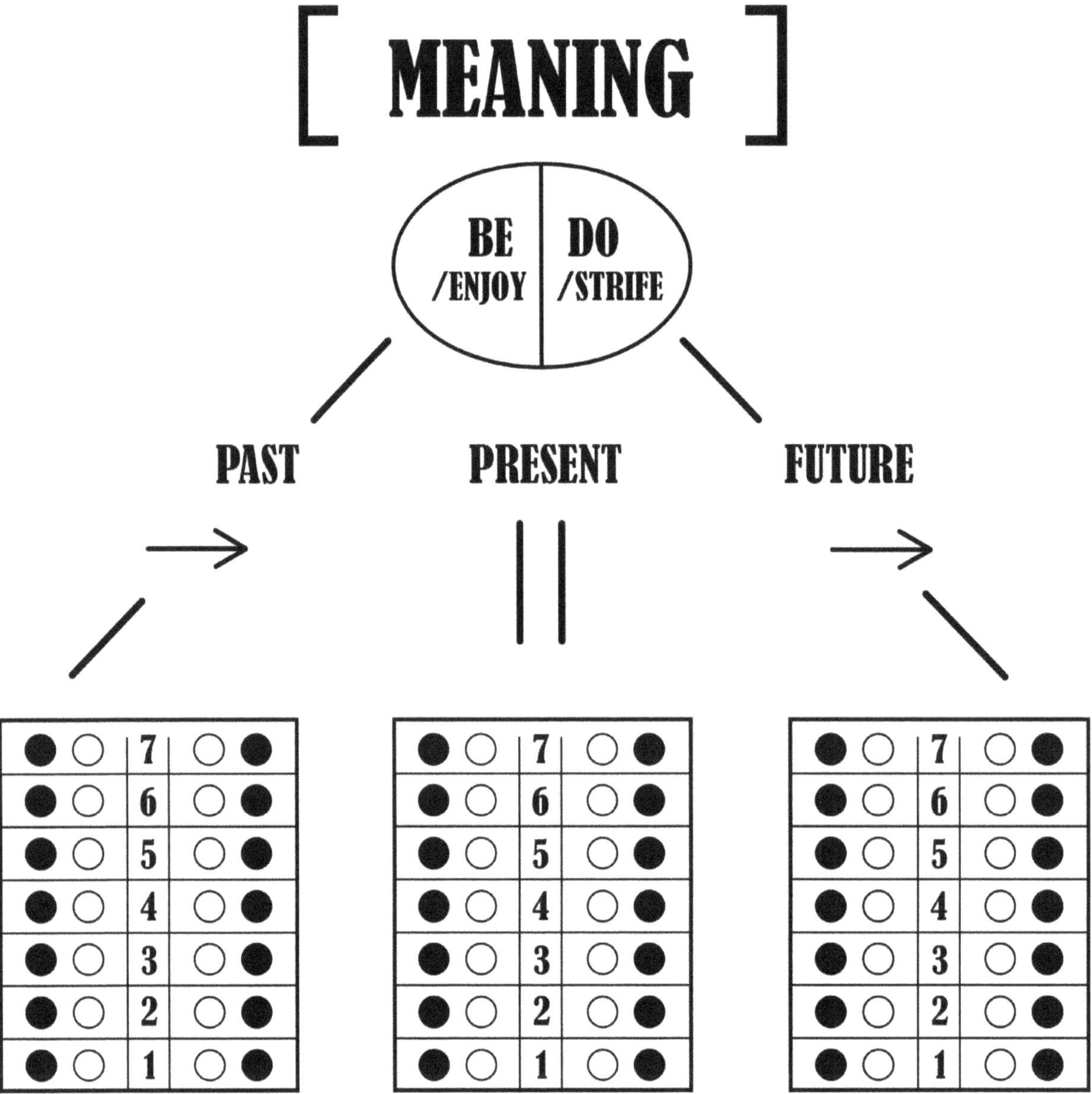

Meaning

Overarching Singularity: Meaning stands here as "The Meaning of Life." When we refer to "The Question," it refers to the meaning of life.

As A Question: Is it a relevant question? No, the question of the meaning of life comes to fruition when we are in a negative perceptual or physical life balance. We can tilt this balance to a positive state through understanding and work. As we understand ourselves and others enough, our meaning is resolved, so even if things are not where we want them to be, it is worth it to pursue life. After that, we can and will look at this balance in our surroundings, but the question disappears.

As A Notification: Even if thoughts of death or questions such as "Is it worth it?" or "What's the meaning of life?" come sparingly, they direct us to the subjective or objective fact that something(s) is wrong enough with our lives. There are a lot of facets that could go wrong. In the later chapters, we will dig deeper into how humans are formed internally. So when the question appears, it signals that we need to reassess our lives.

General vs. Specific: High-level concepts and virtues bring us together. There is a general good and evil, but the concrete pathway to resolving our question will be unique.

As: Be & Do

At A High-Level Perception: It's the balance between being and doing, enjoying and striving. The answer to our pesky question, "What is the Meaning of Life?" is pretty straightforward: it's too much or too little enjoyment or too much or too little strife. If you are inclined towards computers, you can see this as a fundamental binary of 1 and 0, action and inaction.

Zooming In: We can zoom in at different orders of magnitude to determine what constitutes explicitly enjoyment or strife. After a Be & Do dichotomy, the highest amount of Zoom sees the human experience as part instinctual, part emotional, part mental, and an overarching perception. The highest amount of zoom that seemed necessary for me is found in the 'Fundamental Elements List' chapter.

Past Present Future

Timelessness & The Mind: Besides the Be & Do, we have time at any depth you might zoom in. As weird as it sounds, we are timeless creatures. We remember the past to function in the world. We work within the present. We can look into the future with our vision. Even if this vision is cloudy or highly detailed, positive or very negative, a vision exists; without it, we cannot move in the world with any amount of sense.

The Balance: Any of these timeline directions can lead to the question, 'What is the Meaning of Life?' We will refer to this question as "THE Question." All these timeline directions might throw our perception of life off balance. Our past might be bugging us obsessively, or there might be a past traumatic unresolved experience. Our present might be disorganized. Our vision of the future might suffer from unnecessary negative projections.

Past

Questions: Is my reaction to a thought, a situation, or an action negatively amplified by the past? Is my default inner state too negative without an apparent external or medical reason? When delving into our past, the first objective would be to reduce the negative energy we experience today, a reduction caused by understanding. At the same time, recalling and understanding the positive influence of the past is beneficial but secondary.

Technical Past: The past is not physically real in the world; everything that was, every atom in the universe, is now in a different state/position, but you cannot physically reach the past. When looking back at the sky, at the far universe, where we can see the universe's history. What we see there is an illusion created by space-time. Something is happening there as I write this, we just can't see it in real-time. It's a lag, and it's not real per se.

Perceptual Past: How can we know the past is 'real'? That's a redundant question, for we can remember, create stories, tell tales, paint images, sing songs, and write data, but in a concrete sense, the past doesn't physically exist.

Survival & Fear: The inner world contains the Past, being honest and essential for survival. It is fundamental for us as humans and other beings to keep track of dangers so that they survive. For us humans, surviving becomes incredibly complex because the two major fear factors are:
- The threat of physical carnage, damage, incapacity, and death.
- The danger of being outcasted from "the tribe," which would result in being alone in the wild and… death.

The first one we especially share with arguably every being on earth.
The second one adds complexity because of the depth of human nature and the societies we build.

Tribes: In regards to social fear. The complexity increases further in the modern age, where you can adhere to almost any tribe you want, or at least you have vast options. So, what was a simple threat of being cast off from your tribe now becomes endlessly complex in comparison. At the same time, we can adhere to the 'tribes' that we best fit in with, so there is potential to reduce this threat.

Is Our Past Accurate?: Technically speaking, it's almost impossible for our minds to reproduce the past accurately, but we don't care about the technical definitions. We look at it through the lens of the human experience, where the past can be distorted internally by trauma or lying to yourself. The past can have misinformation purposely added as an external tool of manipulation. Even though these realities persist, the past still happened in 1 way: there is one image of the past, and it's just our perceptions that skew it, either internally or from external sources.

Present

Questions: Are we trying to understand why people do what they do around us and the world? Is our own being something that, at this moment, seems out of grasp? These types of proto-questions would lead to introspection about human nature until the answers we find or give ourselves are satisfying enough. These are the holes in our perception that can lead to THE Question.

Technical Present: The technical present is long gone after you stated that "this is the present." What you've said is already in the technical past. The technical present is impossible to perceive as a human because we have a slight lag between what we see, hear, etc., and what has happened, albeit milliseconds, but it's still not the technical present.

Now, people don't work or think like that; no one refers to the present like that, and we will see how that plays out.

Perceptual Present: This is the present that we all refer to and use daily. For example, when someone asks, "How are you doing?" They refer to this day, week, month, three months, year, or year, depending on how often or long ago you've interacted. Especially with the longer pauses in interaction, "How are you doing?" also entitles "What do you want to do next?", which points to the future.

Future

Questions: Is our vision of the future unclear? Is there a plan? Is the plan, at least in estimation, good enough? While delving into the future, having a comprehensive list/vision of the positive elements we envision is essential. Of course, we need to be aware of the possible dangers/downfalls, but without any optimistic projections, our daily positive emotions will go downhill.

Uncertainty: In a way, the future is less accurate than the past. The past is settled, and even if we don't know all the details, it happened; it was set in stone. The future is unclear. You could die tomorrow, and nobody can 100% be sure of an outcome like that. If you can read this, more years have passed by with certainty than the years you know will follow.

Change: Conversely, the future is more relevant than the past. The most dominant reason is that, to a certain amount, our future belongs to us, and we can mold and change it; the past remains.

The Tower: Logical View

We will refer to this system as "The Tower." It is a logical, "hard-minded," oriented map of the inner world. It has its perks and downfalls. For trauma resolution, this is the best way to visualize everything inside. This serves first as a logical, dry list. To understand the overlap between religions, spiritual concepts, and psychological concepts, we will use The Map.

High-Level Clusters

We will delve much deeper in the next chapter, but as of now, this is a high-level overview. In Chapter: Fundamental Elements Lists, we will explore how these overlap and work together in non-obvious ways. The numbers will be relevant in the next chapter, so let's observe the primary subsets.

Instincts (1,2)
1: Danger - Safety, Action - Inaction
2: Relaxation - Tension, Pleasure - Hedonism

Emotions (3,4)
3: Resilience - Fragility, Combativeness - Aggression Toward Others
4: Compassion - Over Protection, Sense Of Belonging - Loneliness

The Minds (5,6)
5: Expression - Inexpressiveness, Playfulness - Disengagement
6: Introspective Awareness - Cognitive Disarray, Delving Deep Into Ideas - Paralysis by Analysis

Perceptions (7)
7: The Perception Of Something Bigger Than Yourself - Abandoned By Existence, Higher Self Of A Path - Nihilism. Note that we can use perceptions to describe our holistic being, although perception is an element that needs to be studied by itself.

The Rainbow Colors (1-7): The fundamental elements list, which is a chapter in itself, is formed out of the visible spectrum of light, or we can see it as the colors of the rainbow.

Yin & Yang (F/M)

Yin and Yang can be seen as good and evil. They can also be reflected as archetypal feminine and archetypal masculine. We shall observe the latter here. All of our emotions have these sides and subtleties.

Yin: Receiving, Having
Yang: Giving, Generating

Linear: We can also view this list linearly,
Receiving -> Having -> Neutral -> Giving -> Generating.
Receiving & Generating is a more prominent manifestation.

Examples of Yin:
A. You have confidence based on 1,000-10,000-X moments where you have prevailed, anything from small daily tasks to conquering evil thoughts to outstanding achievements. It would be absurd to receive 10,000 praises every day. Most of the confidence that is inside of you, you have it. It can also be **received**, but as you can imagine, it is seldom compared with what you already **have**. So, this reception per unit weighs much more than we have passively.

B. In the everyday life cycle, most things in your possession are yours. Although you may occasionally **receive** a gift, this is an obvious example. However, it is essential to understand the weight difference when the systems become more complicated.

Examples for Yang:
   A. Generally speaking, most of our actions can be done from a reserve of energy, which we give up to execute specific tasks by **giving** the energy away. There is also the possibility to "hype" yourself up, create a vivid vision in your mind, and alter your mind state one way or the other. When you press these buttons inside of you, some sort of energy that wasn't naturally occurring comes to life, so you **generate** energy. Generation here is a more costly action.
   B. Say you want to build a shed. You **give** money, time, and attention to make it. At the end of this work, you've **generated** a shed. If it is in progress, you cannot call it a shed, for it has no roof or other mandatory components. Only when it is finished can you proudly say, I have built a shed. Generating, in this case, is a more significant endeavor.

Yin & Yang (+/-)

Fundamentally:
Each element can be useful, good, (+), as white.
Each element can be detrimental, bad, (-), as black.

Generally:
More of a good trait is usually good.
+(+) = (+)
Less of a bad trait is generally good.
-(-) = (+)

Situationally:
Too much "of a good thing" can turn into a bad situation.
+++(+) = (-)
Too little "of a bad thing" can be a bad situation.
---(-) = (-)

Fundamental Elements Lists

Caveats: This EXACT list is not meant to be the end and beginning of all.
These lists, even though detailed, are meant to be:
   A. Practical Guide
   B. Theoretical Foundations that you can build upon
      - Synonyms
      - Metaphors
      - Short Stories
With these universes mapped into your brain, you can expand and contract as much as needed in your analysis of the Inner Universe.

Legend Of The Elements

Usage A: We will use the terms Yin/Yang in the following lists to describe the active/passive nature of each element. These terms follow the definitions provided in the chapter "Yin & Yang (F/M)."
- "Yang" = Archetypical Masculine, Giving, Generating.
- "Yin" = Archetypical Feminine, Receiving, Having.

Usage B: We will use the symbols (+)/(-) to indicate whether the sub-list contains positive or negative traits. These symbols follow the definitions provided in the chapter "Yin & Yang (+/-)."
- (+) Describes positive lists
- (–) Describes negative lists

The Sub-Order Of Elements: Each element as a whole has a fundamental tendency, either toward the Archetypal Feminine or Archetypal Masculine.
- If the element lists start with "Yang", then the element as a whole is closer to the Archetypycal Masculine type.
- If the element lists start with "Yin", then the element as a whole is closer to the Archetypycal Feminine type.

Element: 1 Red [Earth]

Yang: (+)
- **Activity:** Encompassing action, moving, and the need to do.
- **Actively Protecting:** Stepping up.
- **Seriousness / Importance:** Positive sense of urgency.
- **Independence:** Capacity to act independently.
- **Generosity**

Yin: (+)
- **Stability:** Representing both the sensations of being deeply grounded and stable.
- **Security:** Encapsulating being safe and feeling safe.
- **Ease:** A lack of pressure.
- **Settled:** You can feel stable amidst the chaos. Being settled also entitles you to feel safe and cozy.
- **Relief:** Taking a deload, time off responsibilities.

Yang: (−)
- **Violence:** As physical or as words as forms of outward-directed harm.
- **Self-Destructive Behavior**
- **Attack/ON Response:** Without an actual motive.
- **Miserliness:** Represented by being stingy and ungenerous.
- **Recklessness & Impulsivity:** Behaviors characterized by a lack of consideration for consequences and acting on sudden urges.

Yin: (−)
- **Fear:** Encapsulating both fear of physical danger and fear of social threat.
- **Anxiety:** What if something happens?
- **Terror:** Freezing up out of fear.
- **Pain:** You can experience psychological pain.
- **Dependence & Enslavement:** Overly reliant, being taken advantage of.

Element: 2 Orange [Water]

Yin: (+)
- **Relaxation & Pleasure:** Including being relaxed and enjoying non-sexual pleasures.
- **Enjoying Sexual Pleasures:** Manifested through diverse forms.
- **Cleanliness**
- **Bodily Self-Understanding & Acceptance**
- **Acceptance of other Tribes:** Accepting other different people that stem from different metaphorical 'Tribes' stems from an animalistic instinct.

Yang: (+)
- **Sexual Manifestation:** Acting on being aroused
- **Sexual Expression:** Expressing sexuality through various means, such as grooming, clothing, etc.
- **Offering Pleasure (Non-Sexual):** Encapsulating, making excellent food, and offering physical pleasures of various kinds.
- **Bringing others in your Tribe:** Integrating others into one's social or communal group.
- **Being Sensual:** Engaging in actions that are pleasing to the senses.

Yin: (−)
- **Physical Tension**
- **Submissive Sexual Harm:** Being or wanting to be at the end of Sexual Harm & Exploitation
- **Disgust:** Manifested towards one's body or external factors.
- **Personal Discomfort:** Encapsulating inability to enjoy food, not being comfortable eating with others, and inability to relax in social situations.
- **Social Isolation & Withdrawl:** The refusal to be a part of any group.

Yang: (−)
- **Sexual Harm & Exploitation:** Having violent sexual urges and acting upon them without any type of consent, sadism. Or in the form of self as self-flagellation.
- **Sexual Inhibition:** Bland, repressed sexuality observed through various means, grooming, clothing, etc.
- **Generating Gross Unpleasant Actions**
- **Discrimination & Prejudice:** An active impulse to act against groups of people with different physical traits and heritages, such as yourself, "us against them."
- **Being Vulgar:** Displaying a lack of sophistication or good taste; crude behavior.

Element: 3 Yellow [Fire]

Yang: (+)
- **Combativeness:** Encompassing breaking through plateaus and appropriate escalation of conflict.
- **Desire & Ambition:** The emotion of burning passion and ambition for glory.
- **Assertiveness & Intensity:** Do not back down in conversations; say what you have to say.
- **Pride:** Appropriate ego based on reality.
- **Optimism & Positivity:** An outlook that is hopeful and sees the brighter side of situations.

Yin: (+)
- **Inner Strength & Resilience:** Covering perseverance, having passive confidence, resilience, and stoicism.
- **Self-Governance & Integrity:** Having and respecting principles.
- **Social Graces & Restraint:** Showing restraint by being polite.
- **Modesty:** Exhibiting modest behavior, not seeking excessive attention or admiration.
- **Contentment:** A state of satisfaction and acceptance of one's situation.

Yang: (–)
- **Aggressive Overextension:** Overextension that leads to burnout and self-destruction.
- **Hate:** Hating people.
- **Self-centeredness:** Acting selfishly and putting your goals above the well-being of others.
- **Manipulation & Desire For Control**
- **Narcissism:** Lack of a proper ego generates a need to boast about insignificant achievements.
- **Pessimism:** A simplified version of nihilism, "don't even try," "who cares," without a deep mental analysis of the horrible world.
- **Resentment:** Towards other's success. Resentment comes from a series of (half-assed) actions that didn't bring the desired results.

Yin: (–)
- **Relational Dependency:** They cannot form decisions or a moral compass alone.
- **Passivity & Apathy:** Lack of initiative, interest, and indifference towards one's surroundings or condition.
- **Feeling Broken:** Restraining yourself without being virtuous but by being incapable of standing (passively, metaphorically) tall.
- **Suppressing Inner Strength:** Not modesty, but shoving yourself into the ground for no reason.
- **Insecurity and jealousy:** This aspect is more passive than resentment. It targets more what the other person has than what they've worked towards.

Element: 4 Green [Nature/Life]

Yin: $(+)$
- **Emotional Security:** Encompassing feeling loved, cared for, and at home even if you're not physically there.
- **Interpersonal Bonds:** Having friends and an intimate relationship.
- **Inner Tranquillity:** Also known as peacefulness.
- **Sense of Belonging:** Feeling that one is an integral part of a group or community.
- **Ability to Receive Love / Care:** Being open and receptive to the love and care offered by others.

Yang: $(+)$
- **Empathy & Compassion:** Covering being compassionate and understanding.
- **Social Connection:** Incorporating making friends and being friendly.
- **Showing Affection:** Showing enough of it, where and when it is appropriate.
- **Generosity & Giving:** This includes giving presents and selfless acts.
- **Altruism & Human Welfare:** Emotional and physical investment at a higher level. The essence of self-sacrifice towards the good of humankind.
- **Love:** As in showing affection through various means of manifestation.

Yin: $(-)$
- **Emotional Avoidance:** Reluctance to let people get too close.
- **Rejection of Care:** Inability to receive love, reluctance to receive presents, and needing help to accept help.
- **Emotional Suppression & Numbness:** This includes physical manifestations such as overconsumption of food or substances to numb oneself.
- **Emotional Void:** Seen as overspending or other excesses that are geared toward feeling a sense of comfort.
- **Loneliness:** Experiencing isolation and a lack of connection with others.

Yang: $(-)$
- **Lack of Empathy:** Other definitions are compassionless and merciless.
- **Self-Centeredness & Selfishness:** Hyper individualism and uncaring attitude.
- **Getting too invested:** Overcommitting emotionally or physically in ways that may not be healthy or reciprocal.
- **Overbearing & Smothering:** Engaging in behaviors that are excessively controlling or protective to the point of being suffocating.
- **Sadness**

Element: 5 Light-Blue [Air]

Yin: $(+)$
- **Authenticity:** Encapsulating openness, being sincere with yourself, and being optimistic.
- **Playfulness:** Incorporating excitement, feeling like a kid, playful and cute.
- **Curiosity:** Including being fascinated by active listening.
- **Imagination:** Automatic or intentional formulation of visuals and sounds inside one's imagination/mind. The automatic aspect is random creative thinking.
- **Mindfulness & Purity:** Being fully present and attentive to the moment, coupled with a sense of innocence or moral integrity.

Yang: $(+)$
- **Communication:** Covers aspects such as speaking and teaching.
- **Sincerity:** Emphasizes authentic expression, such as speaking sincerely or expressing emotions.
- **Creativity & Inspiration:** Includes dancing creatively and artistic creations like drawings, paintings, and music.
- **Playfulness:** It can be further divided into intensity and cuteness, but at its core, it's about engaging in activities in a light-hearted manner.
- **Amusement:** Includes jokes and laughter.

Yin: $(-)$
- **Dishonesty:** Covers insincerity and fooling yourself, focusing on a lack of truthful interaction with self and others.
- **Disengagement:** Encompasses not listening to others, indicative of an unwillingness to connect or understand.
- **Disregard:** For exploring new experiences.
- **Inner Dullness:** Lack of any form of imagination.
- **Closed-Mindedness:** The unwillingness to consider new ideas or perspectives.

Yang: $(-)$
- **Inexpressiveness** encompasses the inability to speak up and express emotions, capturing the difficulty or inability to articulate oneself effectively.
- **Dishonesty:** Lying falls under this category, relating to deliberate false representation or deception.
- **Outer Dullness:** A lack of excitement or interest; monotony.
- **Excess Seriousness:** An overemphasis on seriousness to neglecting the lighter, more playful aspects of life.
- **Disrespect:** "Being rude" can be captured here, indicating a lack of courtesy or respect in interaction with others.

Element: 6 Indigo [Night]

Yang: (+)
- **Methodical Thinking:** Thinking step by step, thinking with a structure in mind.
- **Concentration**
- **Planning**
- **Being Interested In Ideas:** Interested in ideas that are new for you.
- **Delving Deep Into Ideas:** I am interested and deeply invested in ideas.

Yin: (+)
- **Having a Clear Vision**
- **Profound Understanding:** Of oneself and the world around.
- **Contextual Understanding:** The capacity to comprehend the broader context within which things occur.
- **Introspective Awareness:** A reflective understanding of one's thoughts and feelings.
- **Having Knowledge**

Yang: (−)
- **Unstructured thinking:** Unable to form hierarchies of importance.
- **Unfocused:** Having one's mind all over the place.
- **Shallow Planning:** Shallow analysis of the steps to be taken.
- **Rocky Mind:** Closed to any new ideas, airtight mind.
- **Depthless Interest:** Fleeting interest in new ideas without going deep into the subjects that brought interest.

Yin: (−)
- **Weak Vision:** The possible ramifications of the central vision are also ignored.
- **Weak Grasp Of Self:** Having a frail model of oneself.
- **Poor World Map:** A need for more understanding about how the pieces of the world fit together.
- **Oblivious Of The Inside:** Living in cruise mode without being aware of our deeper selves.
- **Lack Of Knowledge refers** to a general lack of knowledge about any subject.

Element: 7 Violet [Day]

Yin: (+)
- **Being Part:** Being a part of something larger than oneself.
- **Hope:** A high-level perception of hope at a cosmic, beyond-oneself level.
- **Cosmic Fulfillment:** Being the person that you were meant to be, a spirit materialized.
- **Belief In Inner Light:** Belief in your spirit's light.
- **Sense Of Deep Peace:** Having this during our lifetime, and ideally till the end of our physical lives.

Yang: (+)
- **Birth / Rebirth:** Resurrection is a new start for older people or people getting back into the game. For younger people, we look at the birth of The Journey.
- **Guided Journey:** Starting the "The Call" (a call for adventure), the perception of "The Path," and "Perception of Life Mission."
- **Embodied Belief:** "Manifested Faith" is what you believe in and act accordingly.
- **Destiny Actualization:** Reaching your faith's destination and onwards.
- **"Afterlife" Actualization:** Perception of leaving something meaningful behind.

Yin: (−)
- **Existential Void:** There is nothing but silence and darkness.
- **Cosmic Nihilism:** Being consumed by the perception of an "emptiness of space."
- **Existential Alienation:** God/humanity cast you away or "Feeling Abandoned by Existence."
- **Void Of Inner Light:** The type that destroys your passive faith that you are who you are, have a place, and have a role.
- **Endless Abyss:** Nothing led to nothing.

Yang: (−)
- **Incapacitating Despair:** It's too late for me, philosophically blocked.
- **Barren Path:** Barren road of despair, there's nowhere meaningful to go towards.
- **Faith Without Practice:** Belief without action.
- **Quitting On The Path:** Convincing ourselves that there is no Path.
- **Delusion Of Meaningless Action:** The heretical belief that your actions don't matter.

Order of Yin/Yang: This Element is so above our head that Yin-Yang collides, so the order or general tendency is not measurable.

Interaction Between The Elements

Contrasting Colors

The colors attributed to each element are not random. They give us insight into the inner correlation between The Tower Elements themselves and real-world implications. Note that the 7th Element is an overarching one, as it is an Element of itself. We are going to focus on the first six elements and draw correlations.

Elemental Colors:
- Red (1) <- contrasts -> Green (4)
- Orange (2) <- contrasts -> Light Blue (5)
- Yellow (3) <- contrasts -> Indigo (6)

Red (1) & Green (4): Pain lies within the Red Plain's fundamental instinctual element. As part of the Green Plain, love exists. This correlation shows us that without taking the risk of suffering, we can never truly experience love. A perfect symbol of this analogy is a rose, beautiful and thorny. Another more positive analogy is family, which can be seen as a symbol of a great Oak. The tree can only grow in size with a proper foundation in which to be rooted, such as marriage, stability, and common ground. The earth is represented in red, and the tree is defined as life, the color green.

Orange (2) & Light Blue (5): There is a tightly knitted correlation between sexuality and self-expression. Sexuality is the domain of orange, self-expression is the domain of the light blue element, and the intersection between them is pseudo-sexuality, which practically combines the two. The colors you wear, your hairstyle, and the message on your t-shirt are self-expression / creative choices. These choices are showcased in a relationship with your body, be it biologically male or female, which points to a facet of our sexuality. The combination between these two can be seen as pseudo-sexuality, for it's not creativity and self-expression alone, nor an entirely physical instinctual manifestation of the Orange domain. In nature, as a symbol of this intersection, we have pouring rain, which produces minor river falls or accentuates existing rivers, an intersection between air and water.

Yellow (3) & Indigo (6): The Element 6 refers partly to focus, concentration. Imagine an extremely concentrated individual. Our example individual frowns at his computer, trying to understand and respond to the needed operations. A combative 'aura' exists when looking at this individual. There is no peace there, no element of being light-hearted, and "happy" is not the word to describe them. So, focus (indigo) and combativeness (yellow) are combined. For a more yellow-tiled example, we can look at a lifter staring at the bar they will lift. The aggressive 'aura' is evident from far away, but focus is also present, as is tunnel vision. As far as nature goes, you can imagine highly dark clouds roaring with thunder. Even in the daytime, the clouds cloak the sun and engulf the earth beneath in darkness/shadow.

Easy Jumps: This is one of the reasons why it is complicated to isolate elements and study them individually thoroughly. As we showcased in the fundamental elements list, it is possible. Still, when thinking about these elements, our mind can quickly jump between the studied element and its contrasting counterpart, for they are linked.

The Serpentine Pathways

The list of Elements in itself is static. The list resembles a type of map rather than a system of pathways, interactions, and movements. Within this thinking framework, we shall draw and examine part of the movements. This will strengthen our understanding and make it more helpful in making real-world analogies.

Practical Understanding: When analyzing our past experiences, we find a serpentine/zig-zag pattern through all the elements. This pattern is THE pattern mainly used in the Trauma Resolution chapter.

Theoretical Understanding: This non-obvious pattern will also bring emergent understanding, such as understanding the Big Five trait of conscientiousness. The Map chapter will elaborate on this trait and how the serpentine pathway works. Being conscientious is relative to all elements. Some elements weigh heavier than others to generate orderliness and will to work. The subject causes these differences, as well as what needs to be ordered and what type of work is required.

Visual Representation:
(_) will represent element sides that are not active in the pathway.
(+) will represent the active element side.
The numbers correlate to the high-level explanations above and, most importantly, to the following Fundamental Elements List chapter.

Serpentine Yin Pathway:
(+)7(_)
(_)6(+)
(+)5(_)
(_)4(+)
(+)3(_)
(_)2(+)
(+)1(_)

Serpentine Yang Pathway:
(_)7(+)
(+)6(_)
(_)5(+)
(+)4(_)
(_)3(+)
(+)2(_)
(_)1(+)

Chain Events

Inner Chain Events: Our perception is a kinetic chain. We never experience just an instinct, an emotion, or a thought. They are all intertwined AT ALL TIMES.

Usual Efficiency: These chain events are seldom relevant to our day-to-day lives. If someone asks you, "How are you?" as in, "How was your day?" you point towards the most relevant aspect, an efficient transmission of an inner state.

Backfiring Efficiency: Efficiency in our scenario here also means a lack of depth. But this efficiency sometimes backfires. When trying to understand ourselves, we would like a higher-resolution image. Especially when talking about trauma resolution, just the default, efficient summarisation of the most noticeable part of what we are experiencing is not enough.

Pathway Of: Trauma Resolution

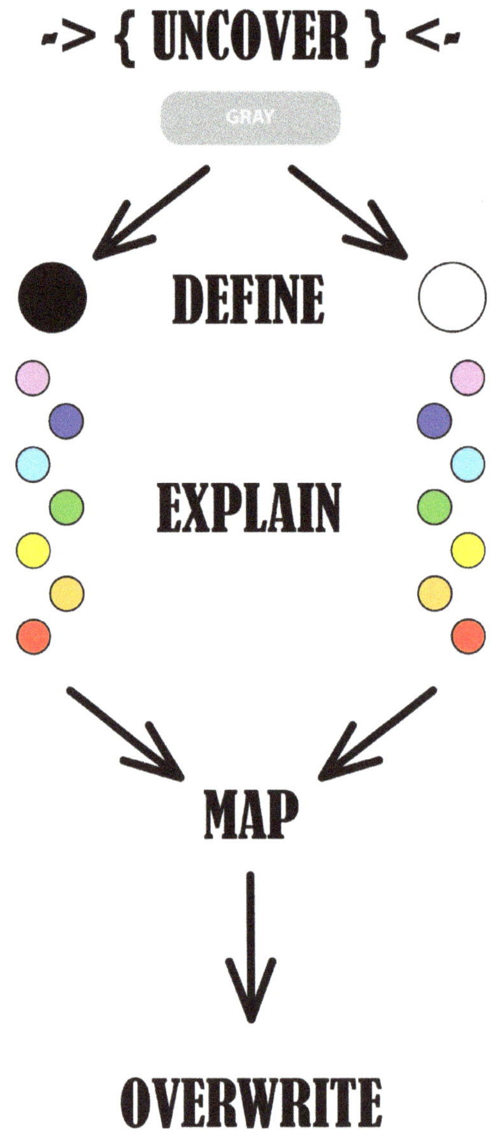

Overview Of Trauma

The Tool

Tool Of Understanding: The primary tool to resolve trauma is understanding. First, we need to know before we can understand. Information about what happened can be clouded by our subconscious so that it doesn't trigger pain. Unfortunately, just recalling the event itself and the main aspects of it, so knowing, is not enough.

Deeper & Different: To fully understand essential events in our lives and pasts, we have to dig deeper, much, much more profoundly. The next step is to understand past events fully. Also, remember that to defeat an atypical inner reaction, we need to think differently, at least for a while.

Defining The Weight

Being Crystal Clear: It is easy to confuse a negative experience or series of experiences that affected us with the strong word, "trauma." Usually, scientists are not great at naming things. They nailed it with "trauma," though. To add to that definition, "traumatic reaction" might be even better. The exact event matters to us personally, but as far as analysis goes, we are interested in our reactions to the event. These reactions are problematic to our lives and bring unnecessary suffering, not the event itself. We shall dissect our response to the event and add piece-by-piece understanding.

Attitude Adjustment: Our initial goal is to determine the magnitude of the problem. The main reason for this analysis is our inner attitude towards the issue. We want to treat serious problems with urgency and importance and self-improvement with a more relaxed mentality.

High Adjustment: Trauma is a severe problem; massive focus and energy are needed to solve it. Traumatic reactions are not something to mess about. They are deep, gnarly, life-disrupting, and, at worst, life-threatening. The urgency of this Quest is High. If you are ready to delve into it, it is of utmost importance that you give it your best till it's done.

Moderate Adjustment: Negative reactions from the past are infinite, but some may hinder our enjoyment of life or our capacity to move forward. See these as a self-improvement Quest. It adds to your life, but it's not "mandatory." Adverse mild reactions in themselves are not disrupting, but we could be harming our life experience as a whole. The potential harm can occur by hyper-focusing on minor minute problems. This focus makes the issues more significant, which would be good if the problem is genuinely worth analyzing, where you would want that level of zoom. Zooming into the problem might yield a negative net result if the problem is minute.

Measuring The Magnitude

Non-Traumatic Reactions: While we are very serious about trauma, this tool can be used successfully to cure bad influences from the past. If substantial enough, these influences will lead to various insecurities and, most likely, unnecessary projections of our future. We can also focus, remind ourselves, and better understand the positives of some of our past influences. Only some things are terrible, and we are hardwired to pay more attention to the negative so that we might overlook the positive influences.

Example A: A parent of the same sex may be different from you personality-wise. You may assume that your later life will be similar to said parent. That projection might make you sad, depressed, and unenthusiastic about your future. Understanding, not only knowing, that you are your being and your later stages in life are your person. The tools in this chapter can help with this understanding.

Example B: A parent doesn't tell you they are proud of you. This is a classical psychological trope. Just because it's widespread information, it doesn't mean that something like this can't lead to issues, or that it doesn't mean anything relevant, or it can't be fixed. Understanding your worth through mapping down your inner world will help overcome this lack of encouragement and overwrite it with positive notes.

Traumatic Reactions: As you will see in the examples list, these are on a scale of magnitude of difference from mere adverse events. These are also the types of events that, at a societal level, will be perpetuated if not fixed individually and as a collective. We are focusing on individual reactions here because you can't change the world if you cannot change yourself.

Examples: When we think of genuine trauma, we refer to things of the magnitude of Violence, Rape, War, Loss of a Child, Loss of a Parent at an Early Age, Divorce between Parents, Especially at an Earlier Age, Extreme Bullying, Extreme Poverty, Natural Disasters. The use of Capital letters showcases the magnitude.

Caveats: People are built in differently. People who are on opposite sides personality-wise will have a very different reaction to those mentioned above. This isn't to say that those kinds of events are ever unimportant, but it's important to understand that people react differently. That is why we are focusing on the "traumatic reaction" and not the event itself per se. This is not a competition of personalities and personal inner builds. We are treating the reactions that negatively impact our individual lives.

Step 1: Uncover

Forgetfulness

Overview: One of the defining 'features' of trauma is forgetfulness. After the event that generated the traumatic reaction, the brain starts to blur out the details. The blockade of memory is not static but tends to grow over time if the event is not innerly resolved.

Manifestation: There are a myriad of possible combinations. These are the fundamentals to look for. FPV stands for first-person view. Another way to describe it is "seeing the memory through your own eyes." In the timeline of our memory, we can experience levels of memory before, during, and after the event. This is not necessarily a linear list, although it can be. Usually, the closer to the critical event, the bigger the memory gaps or unclarity about the event.

Theoretical Steps & Examples:
- FPV full videos with sounds
- FPV full videos
- FPV videos with selectively blurry parts of the video
- FPV video short flashes
- FPV imagery
- There is no FPV, just pictures taken outside during that period.
- No FPV, complete blackout, 0 memories of or surrounding the event.

Concrete Example: Say the event happened when you were 12:
- Anywhere from 8-10 and 14-16, the memories are solid but hazy.
- The years 10-11.5 and 12.5-14 are barely whispering, with some video attached.
- Months before and after the event, around 12, the events are almost a complete mystery.

Functionality & Problem: The mind generates forgetfulness because the events are incomprehensible and hurt too much. In other words, the mind can't handle them, so it stashes them away. This leads to the opportunity to grow stronger and upgrade its understanding of the world. The memories will have a time and day that will be unstashed and fixed. At least, that's the functionality and the reason why this happens.

The Initial Problem: If something like this happens, we work with an incomplete version of ourselves. We could do nothing else at that time, so there is no judgment here. This is the problem in itself with traumatic events. Parts of us must stay locked away so we and the world cannot benefit from these hidden aspects. We humans are complicated beings. One can be immature and mature at the same time. These are facets of our being, and we deal with them till the end. The fundamental difference in our case here is the amount and gravity of that part of us that was left behind. We can be 80% our age and at the same time have 20% locked in the abyss, back at the age of the event. The event was in the past. By the nature of one's timeline, we should be at least slightly more mature now than when the event occurred, but part of us is left unprotected, incapable of growing and moving forward.

The "Let Untreated" Problem: We were slightly optimistic, stating that un-stashing those memories and resolutions would occur. They might never be reassembled and fixed. If we are ready to tackle them and don't have the tools, the will, or the guidance, we will be exposed to any of these:
- A sense of impending doom
- Self-destructive behavior
- Inability to move in the world
- Inability to relax
- Inability to enjoy pleasures
- Emotional fragility
- Emotionally immature
- Unnecessary anger
- Inability to feel loved
- Inability to express love
- Inability to express one's individuality
- Failure to formulate and express ideas
- Horrific vision of the future without reason
- A perception of Abandonment by Existence
- Will to die
- &
- Many More

These effects can manifest as ACUTE responses, "triggers," and chronic perceptions during long time lapses. These untreated aspects not only curse our own lives but also bring darkness to the world.

Remembering

Attacking From Both Sides: As discussed in our concrete example, the closer we get to the event, the fuzzier it gets. That means we have directions to work with. Before the event, leading to the event and current day backtracking to the event. We can visualize it as such:

First Memories -> Close To Event -> ... **Event** ... <- Close To Event <- Present Day

Remembering Through Archives: We will first start with things. Any and every object that pertains to your past and is incredibly close to the event. Sometimes, memory leaks happen years before or after the event, so we are not looking at items that were precisely in place at that moment. This is a heavy, emotionally loaded pathway. The items teleport us to that time and our past selves. Media/Tools/Objects such as:
- Old photos
- Old videos
- Old diaries
- Old objects (trinkets, clothes, toys, etc.)
- Old clothing or clothing styles
- Old entertainment: cartoons, comic books, TV shows, music

Remembering Environments: In the modern day, you can use online tools to take a trip on the memory train. If realistically achievable without significant disruptions, you can also go there physically. The mechanism of environmental refresh of our memory works slightly

differently than the archives. It portrays that we have grown up, time has passed, and we are more mature and knowledgeable. Houses might seem small, distances short, and views less emotionally impressive. Environment variables such as:
- The city, country
- The neighborhood where you lived or knew people from that era
- Surrounding natural landmarks: forests, ponds, natural parks
- Surrounding human-made landmarks: buildings, statues, parks

Remembering With People: This partly overlaps with photos and videos. Here, we add stories you can gather from people in your life back then. From this angle, the pictures and videos are portals for those around you. Those people teleport back in time through them, telling you about their experiences. This not only directly brings data to the conscious, but at the same time, hearing them talk about those pieces of the past, you will subconsciously connect to the type of person they were at that time. The latter is not necessarily evident from the media, so it's valuable on multiple levels. They might also add data you couldn't have remembered if you were too young.

Passing Through This Step

<u>**Concrete Task**</u>: This step aims to have a clear timeline. Digitally or physically arrange all this data that you've uncovered. It might seem more cognitively challenging than it should; it's not that you're incapable. The main point is that the mind wants to forget about these things. You're going, for a while, against the very instincts of your being. Having them visually laid out one way or the other is fundamentally more potent in forcing your brain to remember and put things in order.

    -> Have a visually clear life timeline, especially around the event.

The Far & The Close: The periods further away from the bad event will reveal themselves in more detail and faster. Do not get frustrated if the time you are interested in doesn't appear in full HD and as a complete set of events.

Relative Patience: Even if you go full blast 12 hours a day figuring these things out, a substantial amount of work happens in the subconscious. Sleep is paramount, during which these events will process themselves. Do not be afraid of the possible weird or bad dreams. They, too, shall pass.

Finishing the Step: Things will become more apparent and straightforward after the work is done. Eventually, the Marianas Trench that you were going for will be clear enough. When you can look at yourself in the mirror and say, "<u>I Remember</u>," then you are ready for the next step.

Step 2: Define

Gray/Fuzzy Situations

General Low Zoom = Gray: Relationships and people are complicated. Nobody is 0 or 1, pure good or pure evil. Parents, friends, acquaintances, we see them all in shades of gray. Our brain likes to be efficient. In trying to understand an event, a person, or people's actions deeply, we need this high-cost processing. We need to dissect reality.

High-Level Zoom = Black/White: If we zoom in enough in that gray, we will find pure isolated elements of 0/1, good/harmful. Think of them as pixels that blend viewed from afar, while a higher level of zoom will show each pixel and its color.

Obvious Scenarios: These are the types of attributes that you and everybody around you generally come to a consensus about. Easily observed positive or negative traits. Think of these as primarily objective traits that can be assigned.

Complicated Scenarios: These are situational and can be positive or negative based on the amount. It is not that those people's traits are cookie-cutter, good or bad. We need to dissect how those traits affect us situationally. Was the trait a positive or a negative influence? While focusing on that, we also keep in mind, or in written form, some situational examples.

Example - Archetype Feminine: The overbearing mother (love). The fact that the mother cares is an obvious +. The unfortunate negative result of overprotection leads to this overbearing effect, which is a -. So, this trait of shown love manifests itself as a dichotomy. We need to analyze the positives and negatives of this manifestation as separate entities.

Example - Archetype Masculine: The rigid father (discipline). The fact that there is a favorable structure that is enforced protects us from… doing stupid and harmful things. This element of being rigid can become too much, where no love or affection is shown, where there is no positive encouragement but only punishment.

Random Evil/Negative Acts

There is no gray or spectrum for a random/impersonal act of evil without context (use your imagination), just a big 0. There is no "pro" to it; it's just evil and terrible.

Dealing With 'Random' Negative: What we can do here is understand general patterns of how these horrendous events come into being. It requires more theoretical understanding because we don't have the context, and the complexities of that person are not at hand in any way, shape, or form, so we need to analyze them in general. They appear random at first sight or from afar. Still, we can increase our understanding by having an array of educated guesses about the various possible origins of that evil.

Finding Good In The World: For someone who harmed you but is not known to you, you cannot analyze their whole being and find something good in them. Here, you need to generalize goodness. If a man/woman has wronged you, you must see examples of good men/women in your surroundings. If this is unavailable to you, you need to look up to some people in society that you appreciate or can grow to appreciate, understanding that a particular cluster of people will always contain people who manifest goodness.

Passing Through This Step

Concrete Task: What we need, you've guessed it, is a list. We will use what we've uncovered in Step 1. Take the person who has wronged you and make a clear black/white list of their manifested attributes. Use The Tower for inspiration, but do not shy away from using your own words and descriptions of each specific category. A tip for figuring out the traits involved is to observe both the actions and the inactions. Good and evil are not all about doing something.
- List of people who have wronged you.
- Black/White manifested traits towards you (for each person).

Concrete Task Variation: You might not have met somebody who can expressly point toward your traumatic event and its reaction. In this case, we need to focus on the events themselves. We look at the event as many micro-events, bits, and parts. Try to be as specific as you can. Here, we will lay down some examples.

Black List:
- <u>Natural disasters</u> might bring house loss, poverty, difficulty rebuilding
- <u>Loss</u> might take various forms: missing activities with that person, missing the conversations you could've had, not seeing them reach a certain age, being left alone, and being left with a lack of financial support.
- <u>Violence and war</u> can be seen as multiple bits: lack of personal skill, lack of tools, lack of friends/comrades, poverty, physical trauma, exhaustion, and generalized fear created by being constantly on the lookout.

White List:
- The people who have helped you during and after the event
- The resources that you had at hand
- The skills that you have acquired in the past were helpful

Purpose Of This Task: This will overwrite the automatically generated shade of gray and will bring you clarity about the person or the people involved. After the list is sufficiently grown, we will have at hand targets to break down to the atomic level in the next step. Observing and understanding our situation's fundamental pros and cons is mandatory to comprehend its effects on us fully.

Possible Bad Projections: Isn't good and evil evident? Well, not exactly. Bad, false subconscious projections might occur. There can be unclarity about thoughts such as: "This event made me who I am today." A statement like that is probably true, but there is a subtlety here.

Overwriting Negative Projections: Your spirit, the human spirit, the positive side of you, and the way you choose to define it are the ones who prevailed and brought this positivity to your character. The negativity that you've encountered is not what made you. The spirit, your positive side, brought up light and progress. We can subconsciously make a correlation between bad events and progress in life. We might end up overtraining, overworking, and beating ourselves to the ground, only to feel that negativity again. We might not accept a genuine positive relationship situation because of this fear that without negativity, there can be no progress, and we'll end up in the wrong place again.

Step 3: Explain

Setting The Next Stage

Overview: With our list of events more precise and having more understanding, we will proceed to Step 3. Simply put, we will ask ourselves how those events, people's actions/inactions, and attitudes made us feel. We will take each black-and-white element we've discerned in Step 2 and do it more advanced. We will take that black-and-white point and fully remap our experience across the elemental list.

Considerations: As a cognitive process, this is the most complicated step. There are lists to read and correlations to be made. Do not feel let down if this stuff is unclear from the start. Remember also that when dealing with inner issues, our mind gets clouded. Our inner self wants to avoid these issues because they hurt. So you're fighting two wars at the same time. Understanding the system's logic and dealing with emotion pulls our capacity to reason about how we've felt down.

Focus: Ask yourself what those events made you experience? The first and most apparent feeling/sensation, etc. Our focus here is the first thing that comes to mind when thinking about that black/white dot. Use your own words. This is not poetry. If it's truthful to you, it's excellent work. We will expand on this first batch, but initially, it will be just the first thing.

Use The Tower: With this initial reaction in mind, we will pin our written response through the prism of The Tower. Think of it as a translation between common language and The Tower. It might be straightforward, or some analysis might be required. This first element will be your root wherever it lies in The Tower's structure.

Versatility: Remember that we can have multiple experiences from a single-person event. Our first reactions might be in any realm element. For example, you can feel desolate, sad, shut down inside, angry, etc., as your first reaction. These can be done for both positive and negative influences. We are going to focus on the negative for trauma resolution. Take a break or alternate between positive and negative trails if things get too dark. The positive ones will bring some light to your past. If there are no direct positive influences, think of the Step 2 chapter, Random Evil Acts, finding good in the world and using that to lighten your philosophical burden.

Example A1
Person: Person A
Manifested Attribute: Too Giving -> Restrictions too relaxed
Lead To Event: Teenage pregnancy
My First Reaction: I felt not protected
The Tower Root: Yin 1 Negative (Felt not safe),
  - *Tower Notes: It's inside the instinctual realm (Elements 1, 2), it's a basal instinct of survival (Element 1), it's a passive element, not safe = felt fear.

Example A2
Person: Person B
Manifested Attribute: Lacking assertiveness -> Inaction towards creating barriers
Lead To Event: Teenage pregnancy (same event, other person involved, different black/white points, different reactions)
My First Reaction: Felt left to fend for myself
The Tower Root: Yang 1 Negative (Felt incapable (at that age))
  - *Tower Notes: It's inside the instinctual realm (Elements 1, 2), it's a basal instinct of survival (Element 1), my reaction to it was that I couldn't, that I wasn't capable, so it's an active element which wasn't there.

Example A3
Person: Person C
Manifested Attribute: Callus, careless
Event: Child taken away from my life, cannot be there in the future
My First Reaction: Desolation
The Tower Root: Yang 6 Negative
  - *Tower Notes: Vision is a mental attribute, specifically Element 6. Envisioning the future is an active thing. Yang

Example A4
Person: That Child
Manifested Attribute: Children are good
Event: His existence
My First Reaction: Love
The Tower Root: Yang 4 Positive
  - *Tower Notes: Love is an active emotion, Element 4, which drives you to act out of it. It is an active influence.

Using The Tower

Shattering To Pieces: From the discovered root, your first main reaction was translated into The Tower prism. We will observe the refractions that the root had inside of us. Remember, every instinct, emotion, thought, and perception has a ripple effect inside us. We will take them piece by piece using The Tower.

Serpentine Pathways: Recheck, if needed, the "Serpentine Pathways" subchapter in The Tower chapter. Study both the positive and the negative lists. Sometimes, it is easier to flip a positive concept to the dark than directly look at the negative depictions. Check each Element. What did you experience at that level?

Symbols: (-) means a negative in the yin (left) or yang (right) zone of The Tower. ( ) means an irrelevant zone in our pathway. The numbers directly correlate with The Tower's Elements. References example A1 from before.

Example B1: We've identified "not feeling safe" as a central experience in example A1. In The Tower, it holds a Yin position at element one, as we concluded by reviewing The Tower lists.

(-)7( ) Abandoned by Existence
( )6(-) Vision: the world is cruel
(-)5( ) Disengagement, not listening, not being there (passively)
( )4(-) Not feeling free to express love
(-)3( ) Emotionally vulnerable
( )2(-) Not being able to express my manliness
(-)1( ) <u>not feeling taken care of</u> (the most primordial part of our experience)

Example B2

( )7(-) Something Great could be dreamed about, but it cannot be achieved
(-)6( ) False Understanding: that I am alone
( )5(-) Inability to express emotions
(-)4( ) Loneliness
( )3(-) Lack of power
(-)2( ) Tension, physical and sexual
( )1(-) <u>Feeling incapable of action</u> (the most obvious part of our experience)

Example B3

(-)7( ) Being part of nothing wholistic
( )6(-) <u>Desolated vision</u>
(-)5( ) Shutting myself inside, inner silence
( )4(-) Sadness
(-)3( ) Emotional weakness
( )2(-) Self flagellation
(-)1( ) Inner freeze, shut down

Example B4

(+) 7 (   )   Everything is part of a Greater Plan

(   ) 6 (+)   Positive vision (I might see him in the future)

(+) 5 (   )   Serene

(   ) 4 (+)   <u>Love</u>

(+) 3 (   )   Stoic attitude

(   ) 2 (+)   Masculinity manifested

(+) 1 (   )   Grounded in the world

Expression Liberty: Notice that 'artistic liberty' was taken. Most times, it will not be a copy-past maneuver. Those lists cannot be concise enough and, at the same time, contain all the words or ideas that pertain to that particular subcategory. This is not an exercise of word mastery. You are summoning aspects of yourself from your own experience. Patience and focus are the name of the game.

Inner Summoning:
- **Connect To The Event:** Recall the moments where the black/white dot happened in as much detail as possible.
- **Focus on the inner state:** Observe any instincts, emotions, thoughts, or perceptions that occur inside you.
- **Crystalise:** Try to pinpoint, through The Tower's Elements, what precisely occurred on the inside.

Passing Through This Step

Looping Over: This will most likely be required. This process is not easy. You don't have to "get it right" on the first try. The paramount is that your understanding is growing. Clarity of your situation and inner-world reactions will come through exercise. This head-to-toe representation that you've built will guide you forward to the next steps.

Possible Overlapping Roots: We need a full (all 7) inner explanation of what we've felt regarding the damaging event. It might be the case that we've noted down, say, five reactions <u>to one</u> event or toward <u>one person</u>. By unraveling our inner feelings, we might observe that those five reactions were part of only two serpentine pathways. It is essential to give ourselves time to process, write down, and review our achievements in this step.

No Preset Number: We are not targeting a specific number of reactions. It's your experience; no arbitrary number has been set by someone else. You can have only one explanation "drawn" out and experience the next step, but I recommend trying at least two or three.

More Data, More Results: More drawings of your inner experience are specifically beneficial between Step 3 and Step 4 because, spoiler alert, in Step 4, we will travel through our timelines until the present. If we have more aspects to be aware of while traveling, we are more efficient than re-traveling with just 1 "drawing" in mind.

Step 4: Map

Methodology

Overview: We have written down a list of personal inner pathways with clear origins. This step is closer to daydreaming rather than technical analysis. It's time to connect that past reaction, the fully drawn one, to the present day.

Method: Take one personal serpentine pathway. Take one Element from it or more if you feel comfortable. From the event's inception forward, remember when and where you experienced that element you've described until now.

Note: The internal processing will not be easy just because the technique is simple. You will relive every medium-major effect of your trauma throughout your life till the present day. The purpose of this re-living is not suffering but understanding through conscious efforts the influences our past had on us.

<u>**Abstract Task**</u>**:** Remember where and when you've experienced that element you've described.

Examples: We are going to push forward the examples from Step 3. We are choosing just one element for the purpose of exemplification. This daydream must be done for each of the seven elements of the pathway we created.

Example C1: ( )2(-) Not being able to express my manliness
  - Never actively searching for a girl, a partner. Leading to not putting thought and effort into this specific direction and not caring about it.

Example C2: ( )5(-) Inability to express emotions
  - I interact with people, especially new people, with the handbrake on. I only partially let people know I care for or appreciate them.

Example C3: ( )6(-) <u>Desolated vision</u>
  - Every time I accomplished a goal, it seemed futile; it felt like a thing, a number, an accolade. These didn't improve my vision of the future.

Example C4: (+)7( ) Everything is part of a Greater Plan
  - Seasons cycled, years passed, accolades were achieved, careers improved, and bad moments passed. While all these were ongoing, for better or worse, in the Grand Scheme, everything was a part of something greater than just me.

Realizations: The influence is great because it affected us enough to write it down in the previous steps. We are observing how, throughout our lives, these past influences manifested. We are working to realize that, for example, every time we felt that type of sadness in our lives, part of it, say 10-30%, was rooted in that past event. The situation after the event that made us feel that way wasn't 100% responsible for our reaction. That unresolved past issue <u>amplified</u> our inner state.

How Does It Work?

For Acute Triggers: What we are doing through these deep explanations and mappings is making our traumatic response finer. For example, a baby wants to scratch its eye. It will not be a fine motor function and will most likely be closer to a slap to the face rather than a fine scratch. Likewise, when our traumatic response gets triggered, it resembles not a stimulus but an explosion. By fine-tuning our understanding of the subject, we decrease the size of this explosion. That decrease will become so efficient that through work and in enough time, our reaction will be but a mere stimulus.

For Chronic Influences: Chronic reaction fixes require rewiring. Rewiring necessitates understanding. Understanding requires knowledge (data). Initially, we gathered data about the event. Then, we've categorized our data in binary (good/bad) clarity. Then we've understood what that good or bad created inside of us. Then we've mapped that past complete reaction to the present, and through that realization, we've engaged in re-wiring. This re-wiring starts by plugging the root of that chronic reaction out of our brains.

A wound or a scar? There is a difference between life being "it is what it is" and a traumatic presence. Think of an arrow in your leg or a gushing bloody wound. That is one thing. Rheumatism, which is activated when the weather changes because you were shot in the shoulder at some point, is another. It is essential to understand the difference between the two. Not if, but when our reaction will be but a mere stimulus, we can successfully employ the "it is what it is" mentality and move forward with our lives.

Passing Through This Step

Mapping, as technical as it sounds, is closer to dreaming than to doing math. It is a meditation with a pre-established target. There is no technical benchmark here. The essential aspect here is conscious work, but other types of processing will likely occur. Part of this processing happens spontaneously, especially if you put in a lot of hours in a short time. By summoning these levels of understanding, our minds also process while dreaming, so understanding can occur just by having a good night's sleep.

Step 5: Overwrite

Overview

Action over Thought: Until now, we've focused on our inner world by tearing down unnecessary structures. This step is fundamentally different. It involves physical, practical action. Our actions may directly correlate to our trauma resolution or be slightly more abstract in their meaning. Nonetheless, action is what we are harnessing.

A New Beginning: In Step 4, we've finished pulling the negative roots from our heads. Now, we are planting new seeds instead of those nefarious roots at this stage. This step resembles a behavioral change. If we were to wake up during the weekend and get out of bed at 9 am, we would set an alarm clock; that is an action. In this behavioral change, we are overwriting our past actions of waking up past 11 am or getting back to sleep even if we wake up. The exact mechanism happens with this, overwriting with new neural pathways instead of the old ones we've plucked out.

Defining The Overwrite

Overwrite Event: This step is practical. We will look back at the event that happened to us and go together through some examples and caveats of our overwriting technique. Being a concrete, action-oriented overwrite, it is easier to focus on specific events. Sorry for the strong wording, but we are attempting to overwrite trauma here; it will not look pretty.

Event Example: Direct
Raped
  + Enjoying sexual activity in a positive manner
Abortion (if that created a traumatic experience)
  + Having and caring for a baby
  + Adopting a child
  + Taking care of a pet
Inability to act
  + Setting achievable goals and pushing through them
Poverty
  + Being generous towards the people around you
  + Volunteering, for example, a canteen for the homeless
Toxic/Violent Family
  + Raising your children in a safe, positive environment
  + Being a positive presence towards your friends and connecting with them

Event Example: Indirect
Raped/Violence/War
  + Raising awareness about the matter at hand
  + Sharing your experience
Loss
  + Being closer and connecting with your family/friends
  + Doing something that would make the person that you've lost proud

Poverty
  + Being generous towards a charity

Overwrite Inner State: This is more abstract. We need to figure out what kinds of actions can lead to the opposite of the adverse inner reaction that we've had. We will continue the training with examples from the previous chapter. The "fat arrow," as it is called, is our overwrite.

Example D1: ( )2(-) Not being able to express my manliness
  - Never actively searching for a girl, a partner. This leads to not putting thought and effort into this specific direction and not caring about it.
  + => Putting in the mental effort and working towards finding (personal example) a woman to be in a long-term relationship with.

Example D2: ( )5(-) Inability to express emotions
  - I interact with people, especially new people, with the handbrake on. I only partially let people know I care for or appreciate them.
  + => Talking with people about our passions so that they can get to know who we indeed are. Ask questions about them to understand them better and, who knows, even build a relationship with them.

Example D3: ( )6(-) <u>Desolated vision</u>
  - Every time I accomplished a goal, it seemed futile; it felt like a thing, a number, an accolade. These didn't improve my vision of the future.
  + => Clearly, writing down a Grand Path and sticking to the cycles of effort will eventually lead us there. We already have a good idea of our timeline. By writing down the Great Plan, we can see with our own eyes that our efforts are not futile and lead to development and a better day.

Caveats: Beware of the people you help or try to build positive relationships with. You don't want to jump from one toxic relationship to another, and you don't want to help people who are only there to take advantage of you. Even with the charity examples, ensure they are doing the right thing and are not just a shell for evil to the best of your ability. I know this is difficult to figure out, but keep an eye out.

Passing Through This Step

You Are More Than Before: The above are but mere examples. The core of this step is positive action. You already have the emotion to motivate you, remembering what you have gone through. You are more resourceful than your past self, not necessarily financially but as a person. You have more knowledge, more understanding.

The Focus: The question you should be asking yourself at this stage is:
  => What can I do to make things right?
That is a highly personal question, and no one can answer it but yourself. It is a deep desire for light and retribution, the core of the fight between good and evil.
  => What amount of light is necessary so that your life shines brighter than that darkness? You are your judge. And internally, looking at the scale of good and evil, you know what will be enough.

This final step is twofold. You have immediate action that you can take. At the same time, this will be a lifelong Quest where you will continue to engage in those positive manifestations. To resolve our adverse inner effects from the past, we will concentrate on the immediate actions used as methods for this exercise.

TODO:
1. What positive action, of the same type of those events, can overrule those past negative manifestations
2. Establish a plan
3. Stick with it

Grand Plan: For the Grander life-long plan, we have other chapters that will come next to aid you in this complex and complicated search.
<u>Complex, as in</u> many elements with little interaction but a high number.
<u>Complicated, as in</u> fewer elements are highly entangled between themselves.

Step X: Transcend

Letting the Dust Settle: It's an "X" because there is nothing to do now. Imagine a tank or a bazooka firing at a concrete wall. The wall was broken down, but the path was cleared. The debris, though, is up in the air. It needs time to settle down. All your work will pay off not only in acute revelations but also in time. So this is a message of hope: Things will improve by themselves after the work is put in.

Are You "Done"? You've just closed a chapter of your life, but The Path is Eternal, there is no "End." Your light will continue to shine, and new opportunities will arise.

In Closing: With all these situations taken care of, let's learn more about the world and ourselves!

The Map: Fluid View

The Grand Structure Of The Inner World: It is a creative or fluid-minded representation of the inner world. We will throw in stories and correlations that help the inner world summon that element forward. Indeed, we need clear lists of elements, but if the knowledge is not digested through the subconscious and further, the lists are not usable enough.

The Tower & The Map: There are multiple ways of observing reality. Two very useful extremes are the logical mind and the fluid (creative) mind. The Tower stands tall as a means for the rational mind to comprehend inner reality. As such, we use it to clarify our inner world methodically. But there is another way of simulating this inner world: through the prism of the fluid mind and with an emphasis on emotion.

Every element of The Tower is present in The Map. But by outlining it differently, we can observe correlations that The Tower cannot bestow upon us.

Benefits Of Mapping:
+ We will define The Grand Structure Of Everything.
+ We will explain how that came to be and the logic behind it.
+ We will map physiological structures such as the Big Five Model, the Dark Tetrad, and the ABC Pathological Personality Clusters.
+ We will map other ancient systems, such as the fundamentals of Christianity and mythology.
+ We will observe how all these come together in a higher-level order of structure.

Map On: Main Directions

Short Overview: In this chapter, we describe the basics of The Map, what each zone generally means, and how they modulate.

Top - Bottom: Extremes

Up north, we have the minds. Down south, we have instincts. It is tough to crystallize, map, and understand our instincts.

Thought vs. Action: This map shows that instincts and the mind are on the opposite sides of the inner spectrum. That is why, for example, we suffer from anxiety. Talking to ourselves with our minds works very slowly. Action such as training is a more direct approach. Of course, in time and with enough structure, we can use our minds effectively to control (partly) our anxiety. But it is a long road from thought to instinct.

Indulgence Vs. Control: From the perspective of understanding and controlling our instincts, making matters more complex, our mind guards us from the complexity of the instinctual world. That is usually a good thing, but we wouldn't want the presence of every instinctual craving to come forth in full blast. The problem we can face, and the reason why we are bringing this up, is that sometimes it's important to unlock and work with this level of depth. We don't want to let the wolf roam freely of its own volition, but we also don't want it to starve and disobey our every command. We have to simultaneously acknowledge and fulfill enough of our needs for pleasure while controlling our instincts and keeping them in check.

Left - Right: Extremes

On this plane, we can observe the width of our emotions. Which vary from the West (left) as love and acceptance to the East (right) as aggression and willpower.

Short Overview: There are some general rules regarding exterior manifestations. The left side of the structure should be reserved for human interaction, while the right side should be manifested towards things.

The Obviousness Of Compassion: For at least 95% of human beings, compassion is a general ideal that everybody agrees upon. Different perspectives might exist on how that should be practically implemented and manifested. There are personality differences, and compassion might take various forms. However, most people agree that compassion and love are good ideals that should be cultivated.

The Uselessness of Hating People: Hating somebody yields no positive results in the physical world nor the inner world. For example, we take history's favorite villain, Hitler. We have a person who shouts out with every occasion their hate towards the past character. Let's loop that 1000 times. What did humanity benefit from this misdirected emotion? Nothing.

The Usefulness of Hating a Concept: Now, through understanding, we can direct our aggression, even hate, in a beneficial direction. Let's re-run the same example but through the lens of deep learning. What could have prevented the character Hitler from manifesting that amount of destruction? Everything that will follow is a piece of the puzzle. Maybe if he hadn't gone through WW1, he would have been accepted into art school, perhaps if he had been raised differently and with more compassion.

Redirected Hate Example: Now, our example person, Person A, chooses one of these aspects that weigh down on the final output of history. Person A can aggressively decide that there is a need for action. In our example, action towards the reality that there are people in need of special attention. Without this attention given, without being kept in check, and without having a reasonable purpose in society, people like that can become monsters. Person A has an artistic inclination, so they've decided to open a non-profit where art manifestation is promoted freely and attention is given to those who want to participate. Let's loop that 1000 times. Actions will be taken to create this environment, and humanity will have a net benefit. Person A now hates the lack of a proper environment to cultivate art. That energy went from a person to a thing, a concept.

Hate Things, Not People: With the caveat that, especially with the example given, don't turn people into things.

Moderation: Our example of hating a concept from above is directed at a higher ideal. People do bad things right now. Punishments, limits, and repercussions have to be in place. There is a place for everything. Now, let's look at a smaller scale of daily life. You don't want to be that soft and overly compassionate so that people take advantage of you. You want to be firm, not physically or verbally violent. That is the handshake, the middle ground of our structure's west and east coasts.

The Whole Map Split In Two

Yin & Yang: On the left side of our spectrum, we have the Yin side, the archetypal feminine side. On the right side of our spectrum, we have the Yang side, the archetypal masculine side. We shall look at these two fundamental sides of The Map. Not for the sake of philosophizing alone but to observe and understand mechanisms that we have to deal with in our daily lives.

Repressing A Side: A critical phenomenon is that when we repress one of these sides, it negatively bursts into the opposite one. Let's analyze this statement using its two extremes. The examples refer to archetypes, not sexes. That's why Yin and yang are applicable terms here; they do not focus on biology but rather on ways of being.

Archetypical Yang Character: This person spends most of their day motivated. Aggressive, focused on the task at hand. In their ideal world, they would work nonstop, making goals and striving for their top priority. At the end of the day, though, or at least some days per week, our person needs to rest and enjoy life to recharge. They repress this need for coziness, calm, and relaxation. Their Yang battery is spent. There is no more light in it. That is where the darkness arises. Instead of their inner world tilting towards this loving, relaxing, self-caring figure, they push themselves over the limit to the right. The results are violent thoughts, urges, and a tendency to self-destruct. This result is archetypical negative Yang, for no more positive Yang energy is at hand.

Archetypical Yin Character: This is the most lovely person you have ever met. Always there for you, always listening to your problems. This person puts themselves 2nd to others, and everybody appreciates it. There is a limit, though. When our character needs to be assertive and set limits. There is a place for individuality and ego. Instead of tilting to the right to preserve their time and energy through assertiveness and a touch of ego, our character represses those emotions and convictions. This results in a muddy state of sadness, heaviness, and a general feeling of incapacity. They remain on the Yin side, without positive energy, so the nefarious Yin aspects manifest.

Caveats About Repression: Sometimes, we are forced to push the limits on either side. We could have a toddler that needs attention, even though we are spent. Sometimes, a career opportunity is in front of us, and we must work hard. It is ok to be unbalanced for a while. Significant issues can occur when:
- We forget that we are in an imbalance, and it shall pass.
- When we are not aware of such a phenomenon, to begin with.

Awareness of where we are in life and where we are innerly can be crucial at times, and it can, at the least, be a very positive tool for assessing our lives.

Arrow Directions

Advice given with a confident attitude is generally misinterpreted. Using our map, we shall observe examples of arrows indicating the direction of the inner world.

Heavy Arrow To The Right: War is eternal. It's all about the grand goal. Life's meaning is striving to be your best. Whatever happens outside or inside, you have to keep your intensity in reaching your goals, with no exception. Imagine a motivational scale ranging from -3 to 3+. Say you are at -1 at that moment. The ideas mentioned are at about 2.5+ and 3+. Their purpose is not to set you off balance so you don't enjoy your life and live in perpetual stress. They aim to quickly and efficiently shift your state into a 1+, 2+. They are not to be taken as literal truths that are always true in any scenario. If you have something important to finish up and at a -1 of motivation, you don't want to hear or tell yourself, "Every day, we improve by 1%". You must say to yourself or hear, "THIS IS THE DAY WHEN YOU FINISH IT." Even if it's exaggerated, it doesn't just nudge you in that direction but pushes you in that direction.

Heavy Arrow To The Left: It's all about enjoying the present. It's all about finding peace. Love is all that matters. These quotes direct your inner self towards a more relaxing, peaceful, loving state. They also are not valid in every scenario and manner of life or as a general idea, but tools to pull the brake on striving. If the person is very goal-oriented, then the person has to think of this direction as recovery. You don't want to be burnt up after one month of hardcore striving. You want to prepare and establish a place for relaxation and peace, which leads to recovery and which, combined with all your efforts, breeds the best results in the long term.

Heavy Arrow To The Top: It's all about keeping the plan in tune. It's all about the highest ideal. Every instinct should be kept in check by the mind's control. Dream big. These quotes will make you look at the big yet more abstract picture. They are intended to shift your attention from the daily chores into focusing on the significant philosophical "Why?" of your actions. They are meant to make you observe the progress that happened not this day, week, or month but over several months. They are not focused on the day-to-day efforts. Practicality and the day to day efforts are the ones that lead as steps toward a grander goal. Again, solid ideas and quotes are meant as tools to shift your inner world, not as lifelong decisive correlations.

Heavy Arrow To The Bottom: Be realistic. Everybody has physical needs that they need to attend to. Start today, even if your plan is not perfect. Today's actions are of utmost importance. Stop over-emphasizing what could be and get it done today. This type of quote brings you back to earth. They are meant to push you out of your mind and into practical action. They are intended to quench expectations. Expectations are quenched so that if the grander goal is not achieved at the heights you've wanted, which can very well happen if you have a Grand Goal, you will suffer less. They protect you from stupid ideas that have gone too far without sense and practicality.

Putting It All Together: When you hear somebody online or a parent, a friend, that gives you categorical advice, you don't have to take it personally. From their point of view, they observe that you might need more of one direction. The only reason they use, if they are well intended, which they usually are, these categorical strong ideas is that they are powerful, and if integrated, they work. If you genuinely need that type of unconditional advice, it's hard to swallow, so a little sacrifice of pain and hardship is to be expected.

Context: This happens even on a broader scale. People take somebody's advice out of context, not understanding the concept of direction or arrows. They take it out of context and paint that person as an extremist or an exaggerated figure. They might be a balanced person, just giving the right advice in the proper context. Note that this can also happen when presenting conservative and liberal ideas.

The Curvature

The Map is not exactly a 2D structure in terms of complexity. Imagine this map on a piece of paper. You can fold from the top to the bottom or left to right. This curvature has meaning; it's not only an imagination exercise.

Vertical Folding: The north, the top of the structure as a direction, is generally reserved for open-mindedness. The South is directed at practicality and the instinctual nature of our beings.

Top->Bottom: What happens when you conjure up the idea of "be practical"? Being practical comes with a list of facts and a plan. These stem from the work of logic. Through this fold, we can observe how logic connects to practicality.

Bottom->Top: Utilizing action, we can extract data. Say you have an online business and try 50 different content postings. You act, and then you have data on the matter. The same would go with physical training. You try for three months a set of exercises, then another, then another. You realize through these actions what type of training suits you. Through this fold, we know that action breeds knowledge and where it stands in the structure.

Horizontal Folding: In extreme events, utterly generated or internally produced, a person can experience both aspects of love & aggression at a high level of intensity.

Right->Left: From the angry active reaction towards a place of love, also called "tough love." We can observe this phenomenon in relationships, where the person we love the most can make us angry the most. Regarding relationships, we are not talking about disorders here but a combination of love and anger. Why? Where there is love, there is also the chance of extreme anger. The more you care about somebody, the more you can potentially be angry at them if they act self-destructively. This reaction stems from wanting them to succeed and be well, not out of spite. So we conjure up our Yang attitude, which is archetypal masculine, for them to be well.

Left->Right: From a place of love towards anger. Self-sacrifice at different scales. For example, in a crisis, a mother lifts an object that she wouldn't usually be able to lift out of her child. Out of love for her child, she experiences a massive amount of aggression against the threat. An even more extreme example would be sacrificing yourself for a person you love in a life-or-death scenario. On a lower intensity scale, it manifests when, out of love, we must conjure up aggressive energy to get things done. This inner aggression is not targeted at the person you love but at what upsets them or needs to be done to them.

Map On: Elemental Clusters

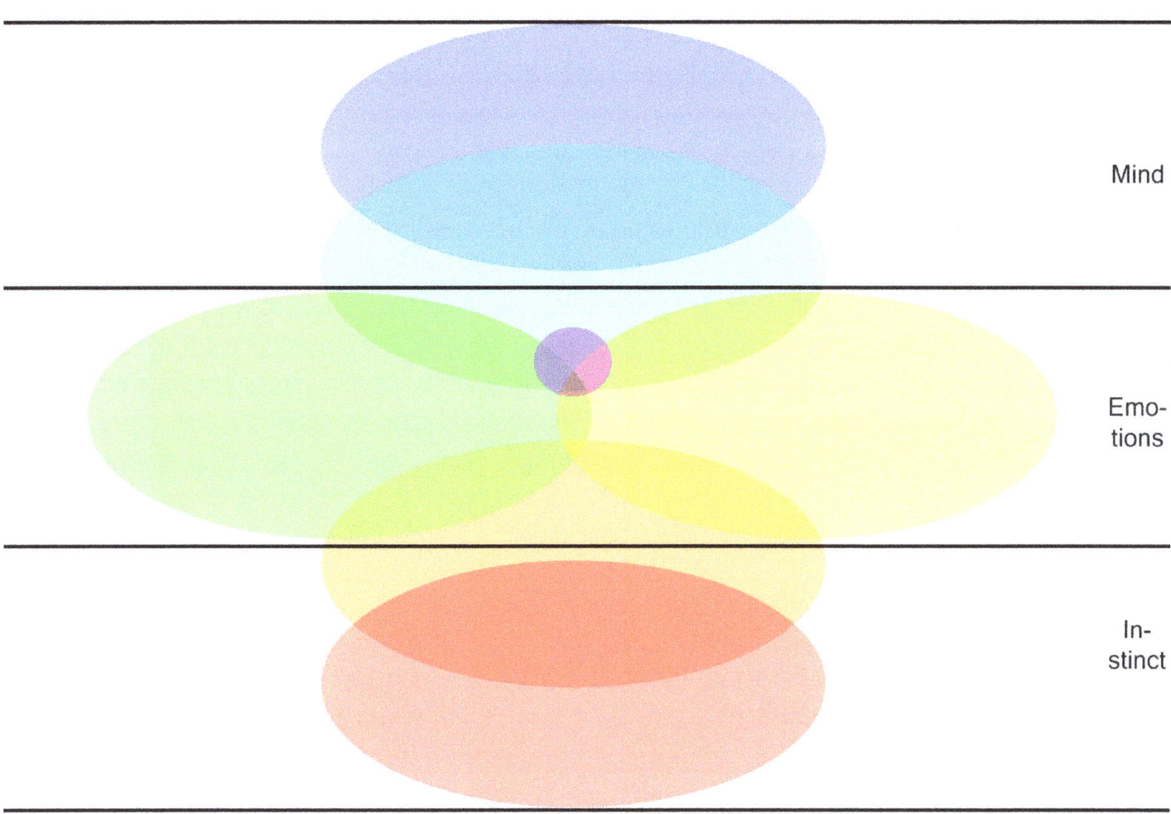

Short Overview: This chapter examines what happens inside each cluster. It is an addition to the "Main Directions" chapter.

1-2 Pain

Pain is a very simplistic experience. No matter its causes, external or internal, straightforward or complicated, pain exists at the root of the being. Pain itself is a Yin substance. You can inflict pain onto yourself or others, but it is passive; it exists.

Causes Of Pain: All these instinctual mechanisms protect us and keep us alive, that being in ancient times but to an extent in modern times. Pain can be directly accessed or summoned through multiple parameters of the inside world. As we've discussed, pain is a Yin phenomenon; it is, it is experienced. In our inner world, in this specific regard, we are either the victim of the tyrant. On the Yang side (gone wrong), we will discover that our very being is inflicting pain on us. The reasons for this self-inducing pain are complex and are to be addressed through therapy or self-therapy (Chapter: Trauma Resolution).

Element 1 - 'Hard Instincts':
- Yin -> Loss (physical integrity of a loved one)
- Yang -> Self-destruction (acute or chronic tendencies)

Element 2 - 'Soft Instincts':
- Yin -> Ostracized by groups: society as a whole, 'your tribe' people close to you. This triggers a sense of loss.
- Yang -> Pleasure excess (which results in self-destruction)

Pain & Depression: There is a neurochemical link between pain and depression. I would also like to add that there is a logical function behind this. Imagine that you are your brain, and sharp pain manifests itself constantly. As the brain, you would like to lower that response but cannot lower the stimulus in a targeted way. You have a big lever at hand, and you pull it lower. The pain manifests less, but so do the other parts of your brain, leading to a depressive state. We could even argue that depression caused by pain is a defense mechanism of our brain so that the mind doesn't implode on itself by the existence of too much pain.

3-4 Origins Of Emotion

By my estimation, emotion does not exist in a void, ever. It is fueled either from the top of the structure (thoughts) or the bottom (instincts) and another particular category. The latter refers to higher-level perceptions of Grand Unity or the existence of a Grand Path forward.

By Thought: Emotions can arise when we think about something. These emotions can be on the loving side of the emotional spectrum or the angry side.

Logic Root: For example, you can be angry that you didn't get into the school you wanted. If that is the case, that is a fact. It is not a poetic interpretation but resides in the hard mind.

Story/Creative Root: You can daydream about past events. This type of emotional summoning is deeply rooted in the storytelling module. We usually tend to make that memory more beautiful or more hellish. It is not anchored in pure logic but an experience, like watching a movie.

By Instinctual Reaction: In the modern world, we are mainly triggered by other people, not nature itself.

Aggression: For example, somebody bumps into you on the street. Then, a moderate (+/-) amount of fight response is triggered. This call to action then goes up the structure into the emotion of anger. Battle readiness is a physical sensation, not emotion per se. You feel energetic and ready when you wake up after a good night's sleep; that doesn't translate to anger. Also, emotion is a more sophisticated compound. You are angry at a form or a person, and the level of anger is calculated through multiple filters. Factors such as sex, age, height, weight, muscularity, stylistic choices, and attitude are all immediately calculated, and these factors modulate anger. Whereas instincts just trigger. You were bumped from behind; you react internally initially the same way, urgency. After you turn around, the above factors modulate your anger and emotions. For example, if you turn around and you see an old lady or a child, your emotions will be downregulated.

Being In Love: For example, love at first sight. Beneath our emotions is an instinctual root of sexuality. Instincts fade rather quickly in comparison to other structures. That's why this sensation doesn't last for long. Sometimes, you can translate that physical attraction by enumerating what you are attracted to, maybe face symmetry, height, weight, muscularity, and general morphology. But there are always factors you are oblivious about in this direction: smell, pheromones, sharper or softer facial features, micro gestures, and micro-expressions. So, this emotion of "Love at first sight" doesn't exist in a void; it has this aspect of physical attraction. Part of the "being in love" fades away in time, but it's still present.

<u>**By Grand Perception:**</u> This can take a more secular form: "us two in the world," "us two," or "the path forward of humanity."

Long-Term Love: We looked at the instinctual root of "being in love," but different pathways can summon the emotion of love. Long-term love is derived from a grander perception. If you are in a fruitful long-term relationship, there is a perception of eternity. In this long-term ensemble, instincts and the mind(s) still work and play a role in the creation of emotion.

Grand Unity: Moving towards a higher level of abstraction. One can experience love in meditation. It can be experienced towards nature, God, and humanity. This emotion is not derived from instincts because there is no attraction or physical observable belonging to a group. It is not rooted in thought, especially logic, though it overlaps with daydreaming.

Grand Path: The perception of a "Grand Mission" motivates us. It's a more dramatic perception, one of the grand battles between good and evil, the perception of "The Eternal War." This motivation is not practical. It is not a logical motivation. If we sacrifice ourselves (part of ourselves) towards an ideal, our sacrifice doesn't meet these criteria. We can get deep and long-lasting motivation from absurdity, from something so Grand that we can barely innerly contain it. Maybe that is one of the key differences between us and animals.

5-6 Creativity vs Intellect

We can think in two ways; with the overlap between said two ways, we have three categories. These types of thinking would be:

+ **Logical:** Step-by-step processing.
+ **Fluid:** Far away connection estimations.
+ **Bridge:** The link that brings everything together.

Far Away Connections: What does fear, an instinct, have to do with perceiving ourselves abandoned by God? What does faith have anything to do with fury? What does the creative mind have to do with sexuality? These are examples of far-away connections. Our creative/fluid mind is responsible for these wild statements/observations. We can derive a practical example from the business world. Where a person, on average, will fail 2-3 times till "they nail it" in business endeavors. These connections have a high probability of being false. So we don't even write down or overthink about most of them. At the stage where they become written, a plan, and then action, we've already checked them to the best of our abilities.

Step By Step Checking: The filter for these wild ideas is the logical mind. We take this idea of ours and try to find structures, reasons, and steps to this madness. That's one of the reasons we have in this book, The Tower. Its purpose is to have a step-by-step logical structure so that, regarding our inner world, we can trace unexpected or mysterious feelings or other reactions that we manifest.

Linking The Two:
- **Just Step By Step:** We cannot attain leaps in our understanding by only using our step-by-step guide. This reduces the probability of great ideas and revelatory experiences.
- **Just Far Away Connections:** By using too many far-away unchecked connections, we start believing idiotic ideas that have no purpose, spiraling into psychological madness. Psychological madness means that you cannot fix it with a pill. It's just how you allowed yourself to think for a long time.
+ **Bridging:** Bridging doesn't mean staying mild in using one of these two ways of thinking. We let our dreams be significant and use our logic thoroughly, but we ensure the use of both. For our best use of the two minds, we need a combination. Otherwise, we slug away in our evolution or go mad with absurdity.

Map On: The Big Five (Psychological)

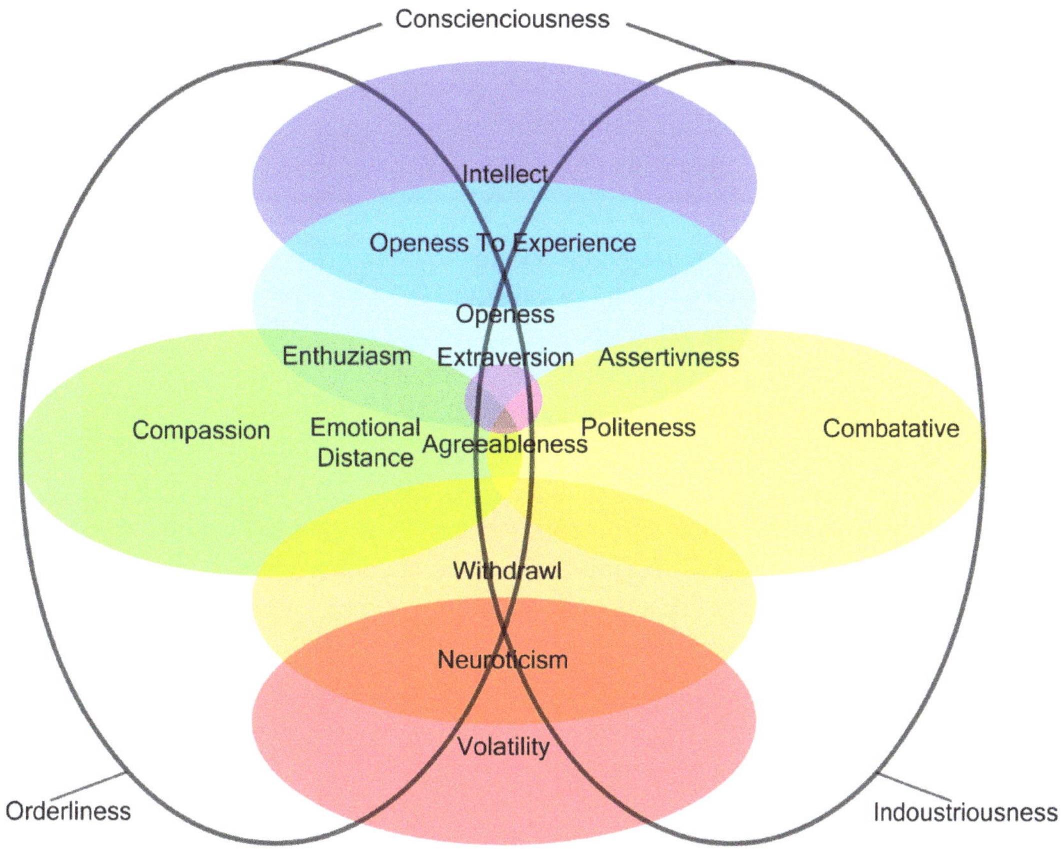

Overview

What Is "The Big Five": It describes personality traits. The Big Five is a personality model that has been extrapolated by gathering cross-cultural data responses from users. It showcases that across the globe, people tend to describe others and themselves in five big dimensions. Each dimension creates clusters of people who share traits. These five big dimensions have two subdimensions that help us better navigate this system's details.

Specific Version Analyzed: This caveat must be added for the technical, psychologically savvy reader. We will describe the version of this structure based on research by Jordan Peterson, Colin DeYoung, Lena Quilty, and Jeremy Gray. Their version is a close alternative to the original Big Five system.

Integration: We will tackle positioning these traits in The Map and mention The Tower. The element numbers refer to The Tower chapter. With this overlapping, we will observe exciting correlations between different ways of viewing the inner world.

Ambivalent Reality: Every trait at its extreme has apparent pros and cons. None of the characteristics are inherently good or bad. I will add my take on how the extremes could be named to understand the pros and cons better.

Open Mindedness

Intellectuality
Map: Up North
Element: 6

High In Trait
Description: Intellectuality is the general tendency to be interested in ideas and to process and understand data. It is closely related to logic and is serious in nature. This is the hard mind. Refers to the step-by-step processing mind.
Pros: People with this trait tend to gather much information while moving through life. They are also good at planning because that requires logic.
Cons: Temptation to overanalyze a subject and act too little. Analysis by paralysis. A general con is that even if these types apply their thinking constructively, they tend to succeed later in life than a more practical thinker. Examples include "How long does it take to become a doctor/lawyer/scientist/engineer?". By the very nature of intellectuality, these types of work take a very long time to mature and become functional at a high level.

Low In Trait
New Term: Practical Thinker
Description: Practical thinkers are the administrator types. They do not tend to overthink the system at hand but execute it.
Pros: People not obsessed with ideas tend to be more pragmatic. If the system they work within is excellent or good enough, the nuts and bolts keep the machine rolling. People who choose more practical jobs such as carpenter, cook, or electrician will find success earlier in their lives and can more easily have a family at an earlier age.
Cons: Sometimes, innovation is necessary. People who take the system at face value might need help shifting their behavior and adapting to the changing nature of the world.

Creativity
Map: North
Element: 5

High In Trait
New Term: Fluid mind
Description: Creativity is a need for self-expression, making far-away connections between subjects, fascination, and random thought.
Pros: A person high in this trait will have an urge to create, to manifest. They can keep it shut for a while, but eventually, it needs to be released. They can generate new angles of observation. They tend to think about wacky/new business ideas. Their perception of the Divine, higher power tends to have multiple shapes and forms.
Cons: Chaos, disarray, and the possibility of believing in wildly untrue ideologies. Creativity is hard to monetize, so the need to create might remain just a hobby. Wild conspiracy theories are also generated through the random thinking process.

Low In Trait
New Term: Crystalized mind
Description: A person resistant to changes. Dogmatic belief that preserves the past.
Pros: Their beliefs strongly resemble the religion they were born within, which allows old teachings to be passed down through generations.
Cons: Can become ideologically too stiff. Where the world, from time to time, does genuinely change, they tend not to accept that some parts of dogma should be overwritten.

Extraversion

Enthusiasm
Map: North-West
Element: 5+4

High In Trait
Description: Maybe the closest inner attribute we could name is "positive emotion." It is pure, non-destructive, and serene.
Pros: Being happy, being optimistic, projecting a positive outcome to our chosen direction.
Cons: High expectations, which can lead us to disappointment. These types of expectations can happen in any and every aspect of our lives. Intimate relationship-wise, it can lead to jumping necessary relationship-building steps. Examples of the latter would be moving together too soon or getting engaged too soon.

Low In Trait
New Term: Emotionally precautious
Description: Reserved, partially inhibited emotion, neutral emotions.
Pros: If the event that we could be enthusiastic about has a low logical probability of turning out well, we can modulate our inner state so that if things don't go our way, we can deal with it quickly. People who exhibit this trait are generally more emotionally stable, with fewer ups and downs.
Cons: Not enjoying life, being emotionally unmovable like a stone. Having this trait in excess can make us so emotionally precautious that even if, for example, our achievement has been validated several steps along the way, we still feel nothing. We are allowing ourselves to feel something only three months after the confirmation, where not much positive emotion regarding the positive change in our lives has occurred.

Assertiveness
Map: North-East
Element: 5+3

High In Trait
Description: The ability to speak our minds, for better or worse, and stand up for ourselves.
Pros: A person like this will not question what they could have said in XYZ situations. They are always ready to make their part of the argument audible.
Cons: Excess self-expiration when interacting with other people can leave a void of listening capacity. We can become a stone wall, where the things said to us just bounce back into the cosmos.

Low In Trait
New Term: Restrain
Description: A more patient person who listens first than speaks.
Pros: A lack of unnecessary harmful exposure. Just because you have an idea doesn't always mean you should vocalize it.
Cons: Listening and thinking, of course, is a positive narrative. At its extremes, it can lead to a pile of unexpressed feelings or ideas, leading to bottled-up emotions and sentiments.

Agreeableness

Compassion
Map: West
Element: 4

High In Trait
Description: Love, emotional understanding, empathy, warmth, and generosity manifested as material or as emotional implications and time spending.
Pros: This is generally a very highly valued attribute in human interaction. In intimate relationships, it's one of the most sought-after values. In general societal terms, this is the definition of "a good person."
Cons: Some people grasp the value of this attribute but might be tempted to forget that it is not the only relevant thing in life and human interaction. They can also become afraid of the East side of The Map, of being even slightly combative. This leads to Yang's repressed emotions, which jump ship to the other side as sadness and muddy emotions.

Low In Trait
New Term: Emotionally Distant
Description: When you meet a person for the first time, or when you meet somebody in a more work-related severe environment, the relationship starts with a low level of emotion.
Pros: People who tend to be like this tend to hold more energy in themselves. Listening and being close to somebody is draining, even if it helps the other person. An attitude like this gives more room for logical processing, which is valuable, especially in work-related issues.
Cons: This work-like emotional distance is not sought after with close friends and in an intimate relationship. You cannot honestly know somebody if you never open up to them; that's what you genuinely want in these close relationships.

Politeness
Map: East
Element: 3

High In Trait
Description: Politeness can be subtle, such as how you express yourself at work, or it can manifest more brutally, as it happens in the military. Politeness, from a direction from West to East, is the last gate until conflict becomes ugly.
Pros: Discipline, knowing where you stand, and controlling aggression. For the more subtle manifestations, we look at elegance in our approach. We can be assertive and impolite or say what we must say more pleasingly.

Cons: We manifest this in more formal environments so that order is maintained. It would be weird and distant to engage with our friends too politely. Imagine texting your friend: "Mister Sav, I truly hope this has been a luminous and productive day. Would you like to spare 2 hours of your time this afternoon to bring us up to date with each other?". With people you are comfortable with, more often than not, politeness gets thrown out of the window, so too much of it in the wrong scenario is awkward and distant.

Low In Trait
New Term: Combative
Description: Impolite is a word with a negative connotation. Being combative is on the other side of the spectrum regarding politeness. It has its uses and roles to play in life.
Pros: Competing in any challenge/sport/goal with other people. The usefulness of this becomes even more apparent when we consider being combative with a self-proclaimed goal toward something we wish to accomplish. The very element of fire brings actual change in our lives.
Cons: Outside these competitions, with others, with outer things, or with ourselves, combativeness becomes a challenge and awkward trait in social interaction. Not every talk is a fight. People who are very high in this trait tend to want "to win" at everything, even when it isn't essential.

Neuroticism

Withdrawal
Map: South
Element: 2

High In Trait
New Term: Withdrawal / Tense
Description: The best analogy I've found for the personality aspect of "withdrawal" is a scaredy-cat-like behavior. It's not explosive; it's subtle, such as a cat being cautious towards something it doesn't know, retreating, or getting closer softly and gently. This attribute seems closely attached to social interactions as an instinctual root.
Pros: One can have 1000 acquaintances but no friends. Spending time randomly mingling with people you do not connect with can be wasteful. This avoidance can also help a person focus on their day-to-day goals and bring structure to their lives. There is also an element of tension attached to it. We can achieve certain types of goals through this tension and restriction of pleasures.
Cons: Avoiding mingling with people, resulting in a smaller social circle than personally desired over the years. An inability to express pseudo-sexuality as it is. For example, you would like to wear a tiger print shirt, but this type of cautiousness makes you choose something bland, even if you would prefer it less for the day. The tension aspect can become exaggerated, where we don't allow ourselves to relax, leading to burnout or a general apathy towards life caused by lack of pleasure.

Low In Trait
New Term: Physically Relaxed
Description: A relaxed person, especially physically, doesn't experience the wish to withdraw from society. The person is comfortable while both being alone and with others. There is no real reason to fear these interactions because it doesn't change the state of tension.
Pros: Outgoing, having people enter and leave their lives without much inner disturbance.
Cons: These easy ins and outs of people might create superficial relationships.

Volatility
Map: Bottom South
Element: 1

High In Trait
New Term: Volatility / ON State
Description: This is in the realm of the most primordial instinctual reactions. People high in this trait are primarily ON or ready for something wrong to happen. This ON is a sense of urgency that lurks around most of the time for them.
Pros: People like this tend to observe threats sooner than others. This type of energy is welcomed in some situations, such as taking care of an infant. This inner state extends to other societal roles, such as security. For example, if you are an IT security expert, you must be somewhat paranoid and very alert to every possible action of a potential attacker; that's your job.
Cons: Only some of their observations about potential threats are accurate. They suffer the fear of both real threats and those who are off-target. Too much of a state of urgency compared to what the environment brings forth is called anxiety.

Low In Trait
New Term: Stable / OFF State
Description: These are the people who are calm during the storm. Whatever comes their way, they will not agitate themselves or others around them.
Pros: In our modern developed society, there are few actual high-urgency dangers. People who are ON are appreciated for raising the flag, but usually, people who are more steady and cool-headed will find the appropriate solutions and implementations for said issue.
Cons: This OFF state can also be exaggerated, for example, having clear physical health symptoms and just ignoring them when later they turn out to be a big issue or even, God forbid, irreversible.

Conscientiousness

Complexity: This is by far the most complex and complicated trait. It contains every Element on the Yin or Yang sides, depending on the case. We shall use The Tower to get all the details step-by-step.

Orderliness
Map: All Towards The West
Element: 1-7 Yin Serpentine Pathway

High In Trait
Description: Order comes at multiple levels. It is part of the physical arrangement of things, to the cleanliness of things. It is part of emotional restraint. It is part of values and hierarchies. It is part of the high-level perception of good and evil.
- Element 7 Yin: We are part of Something Greater than ourselves - passive.
- Element 6 Yang: We check and make plans - active.
- Element 5 Yin: We want things to be cute and in place - passive.
- Element 4 Yang: We want order so that we can take care of ourselves and others - active.
- Element 3 Yin: Moral values and rules should exist - passive.
- Element 2 Yang: Tastefully manifest our bodies through the prism of society - active.
- Element 1 Yin: Physical order should exist - passive.

Pros: Clean, tidy, disciplined, having long-term plans, planning for the future.
Cons: Tendency towards obsession, making everybody else uncomfortable and stressed, and forgetting that life has two main aspects: Enjoyment and Struggle.

Low In Trait
New Term: Free
Description: A person who puts the structure and norms of their house, relationships, and societal hierarchies on the back bench.
- Element 7 Yin: We are a bunch of atoms, and everything is random - passive.
- Element 6 Yang: We look at the high-level plan without detailing - active.
- Element 5 Yin: Messy, creative, seems disorganized but knows where everything is - passive.
- Element 4 Yang: We feel love and affection rather than focus on the exterior - active.
- Element 3 Yin: Only some crucial rules are mandatory, less stiff - passive.
- Element 2 Yang: Overcare about our appearance, toned down - less active.
- Element 1 Yin: Being overly tidy is stressful, but keeping energy - passive.

Pros: Tendency towards being relaxed, not allowing outside changes to disturb us, being malleable regarding social structures, rules, and norms.
Cons: Letting chaos reign over our vision of what social norms should be and what principles should be respected. Too much chaos leads to anxiety.

Industriousness
Map: All Towards The East
Element: 1-7 Yang Serpentine Pathway

High In Trait
New Term: Industriousness / Hard Worker
Description: A person works with multiple inner systems to output work into the world. To be more specific, all the elements are used. Somebody who is genuinely into WORK MODE will have the inside:
- Element 7 Yang: The Path of improvement is Eternal - active.
- Element 6 Yin: Trusting a made plan - passive.
- Element 5 Yang: Expressing our thoughts about what to do - active.
- Element 4 Yin: Taking others nearby into account passively at a minimal need-to-interact basis - passive.
- Element 3 Yang: Will, aggression - active.

- Element 2 Yin: A state of physical tension - passive.
- Element 1 Yang: A sense of urgency, of NOW, an ON state - active.

Pros: Results, progress, maximizing our potential. You can be born with a high degree of this trait, but it can also be imbued by having a plan and slowly increasing one's work capacity through personal effort.

Cons: This attitude can lead to burnout, overkilling ourselves for a 10% increase in performance that might not matter, and forgetting to manage stress and effort. For example, a pre-planned deload of 1-2 weeks after a cycle of 8-12 weeks of effort is deleted in hopes of getting more out of ourselves. This leads to either non-ideal long-term results or a lack of satisfaction when we do achieve our goals. Tunnel vision, forgetting about the people around us.

Low In Trait

New Term: Laid Back

Description: A person who lives without focusing on objectives but instead on enjoying the moment.

- Element 7 Yang: We are going towards our Grand Direction, but it may change because we, the others around us, or the world might change - active.
- Element 6 Yin: We'll see when we get there mentality - passive.
- Element 5 Yang: Discussing off-topic, human-centered, entertaining conversations - active.
- Element 4 Yin: Taking others nearby into account - passive.
- Element 3 Yang: Low emotion, slow grind - active.
- Element 2 Yin: Just enough tension so that we can work - passive.
- Element 1 Yang: Moderate effort - active.

Pros: Cooldown, the recovery side of effort management.

Cons: Being lazy, not having a plan, not achieving anything meaningful, and not striving for the best possible subjective outcome.

Final Notes

The terms are coined in The Big Five so that some directions and extremes are described as good and the other sides of the traits as bad. Indeed, there is a general tilt and truth to this order. Generally speaking, it's better to:

- (Neuroticism) Not experience fear
- (Agreeableness) Be nice
- (Extraversion) Enjoy life
- (Open Mindness) Learn and be creative
- (Conscientiousness) Work hard and consistently

However, as we saw in our analysis, there is a place for the opposite side of these traits. A place that is important in our lives and in our society as a whole.

Map On: The Dark Tetrad (Psychological)

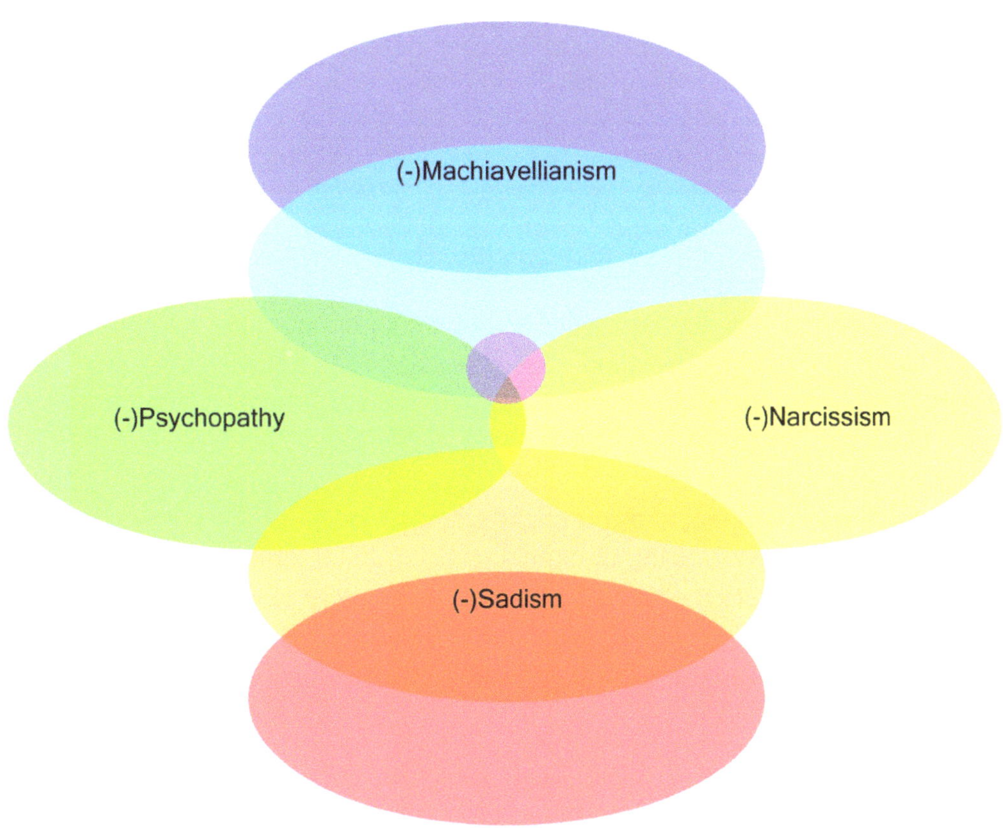

Overview

Points Made: The Dark Tetrad is a psychological system that focuses on pathological traits. We will describe what the traits mean. Where do these traits stand in The Map? What are the roots of these traits, and what are the most crucial aspects that make them manifest?

Focus: It's important to note here that the vast majority of people have bits of these traits. We rather refer to them as a Dark Tetrad when their manifestations are obvious and hurt the people around them. Here, we observe how they manifest in us, why they exist, and what we can do about them. When talking about 'solutions,' we mainly target low-moderate amounts of these traits we manifest ourselves. These 'solutions' are not meant to be considered society-wide solutions but tools for personal reflection.

Trauma & Deeper Analysis: Part of the trauma resolution is understanding evil. This chapter is meant as an overview of various manifestations of evil. If, through The Tower, you cannot yet fathom enough why a person would do such horrible things, then understanding these evil traits can significantly boost your understanding. You can figure out if, in your situation, the person who did you wrong manifested one of these traits. Most likely, that is the case. This overview might not be enough by itself. So, if you need more information on a specific trait, explore as needed.

Flamboyant Examples: We will give examples from fantasy and comic book characters. In these imaginary universes, the characters can easily be wildly exaggerated, portraying these traits in an obvious manner.

Machiavellianism

Position: North
Elements: 6+5
Root: Extreme mental detachment
Description: The Mind in Isolation from the rest of the inner structure. In terms of character, think of the hidden brain of the operation. This character does not wish for glory. This character isn't personally trying to manipulate people. This character is not hands-on. Think of a little mischievous, scheming, plotting creature with few qualities than its mind.
Manifestations: Unscrupulous decision-making, wholly cold vision of others. Cheating and manipulation behind the scenes, spawn out of these attitudes.
Solutions: Pay close attention to the moments when you feel empathy and love. Remember these moments when you are making a plan and summon that ounce of compassion that will align your strategy with others' lives. Don't let the infinite openness of the mind diminish the fact that there are moral values and principles on which the world and social hierarchies are built.

Narcissism

Position: East
Element: 3
Root: Lack of a proper ego, of earned pride.
Description: This is our flashy type who will squeeze out every ounce of admiration they can from others. The inner pride of this character is frail, but the outside mimics it as enormous and glorious. This lack of established self-esteem breeds this desire always to top off their received admiration. These manifestations stem from a bottomless pit of insecurity.
Manifestations: These types hate it when somebody else takes the spotlight. They will become jealous and try to bring the people around them down so that they can come out on top. They would instead do that instead of focusing on improving themselves. These manifestations are not limited to people they don't know but to the very core of their relationships, yes, intimate ones, too.
Solutions: Being aware of what you are good at in life. Being aware of what you are bad at in life. Understanding that you cannot fulfill every role in society, but you are limited to your own attributes. Noting down, being aware of your abilities and what you know will also bring to the foreground all the vastness of your incapacity as an individual human being. Noting down your weekly efforts creates a sense of genuine pride that doesn't need much, if any, validation from the outside world.

Psychopathy

Position: West
Element: 4
Root: Lack of compassion/love.
Description: There exists a robust literature on psychopathy. When analyzing the root, though, we understand that all the negative manifestations would be wholly or partly dissolved if enough compassion/love were present.
Manifestations: We shall focus on the root when talking about the manifestations. Impulsivity: if that impulsive action hurts yourself, we observe a lack of self-love. If the impulsive action hurts somebody else, it's a lack of compassion. The lack of fear stems from the disregard for others. Why would you fear repercussions if you don't care about others? The same applies to guilt; why would you feel guilty if you did not care? Caring which is in itself a form of love.
Solutions: Most people are not psychopaths, so most people feel a certain amount of care, compassion, and love. There are guided meditations, or you can make up your own, focusing on feeling love and connection. The focus is on the middle chest area while staying comfortable. If you struggle with experiencing this feeling, focusing on nature and connecting with it is more accessible as a first step. Then you can move on to your family/friends, then to all the people you know, and lastly, you can feel love towards the world itself. Put on some soothing music, and get closer to that general feeling of love with each meditation. By being in touch with this side more, it will be less likely to manifest these negative traits of psychopathy.

Sadism

Position: South
Elements: 2+1
Root: Pleasure & Violence
Description: This is a highly visceral trait. It reigns in the South of The Map, in the instinctual lands. When thinking and observing sadism, we must pay close attention to the more subtle manifestations to fully understand this notion. Yes, there are clear-as-the-sky manifestations, such as sexual sadism or torture, but those are obvious. "Fun Fact": animals such as our close genetic relatives, the chimpanzees, were observed undertaking sadistic & violent actions just for the sake of it. For example, when seven chimps face one or two, they clearly win, but they tear apart and mutilate their opponents before delivering the decisive strikes. It makes you wonder what the hell is in our unconscious animalistic brains.
Manifestations: We will look at the more subtle variants of sadism, for the physical ones are too obvious even to analyze. When somebody trolls or bullies a specific person online, they are trying to inflict pain. It is not bodily pain, but the parts of the brain capable of signaling pain are in motion even if the cause is not physical. Let's take mocking, bullying, and tearing people down. In this case, it is not so that the bully receives "more glory and glamor." Narcissism and sadism can coexist, but they are isolated aspects of a more complex psychological system. They enjoy the other person being hurt. Their status or place in the world is irrelevant; "I just want to make you hurt" is the type of attitude specifically in sadism.
Solutions: This is an instinctual pleasure. Instincts are the most volatile and short-lived out of the inner realm's main sides. The solution here is 'mindfulness'. Being aware of your desire to feel that pleasure of hurting. Taking several deep breaths, thinking about peace or

being on top of a mountain. Enough of these 'cooling' off exercises will help stop the urge to punish others.

Map On: The ABC Clusters (Psychological)

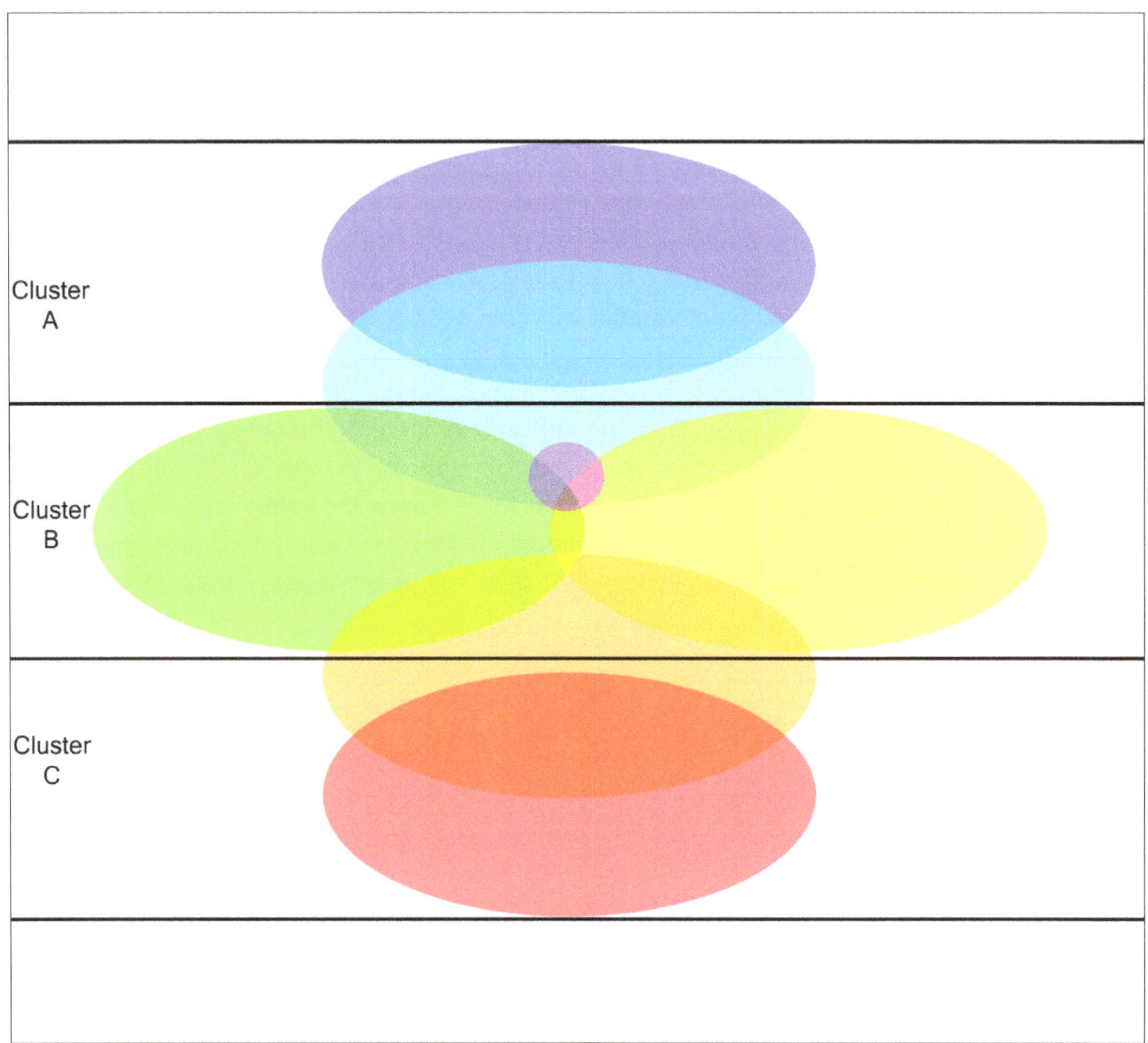

Overview

As Traits & Disorders: These traits have a dual nature to them. On the lower ends of the spectrum, they resemble personality traits more; on the higher ends of the spectrum, they become problematic, so we call them personality disorders. You might realize that you have partial, mild - very mild manifestations of several of these traits; those are not 'disorders.' A good rule of thumb is when a trait gets in the way of you measurably living your best life. Then, it falls closer into the disorder zone.

Personality Traits: They help us understand our negative actions and reactions. Note the word personality. Although the focus is on the negative, we will outline the positives of each trait. By understanding these positives, we can better rationalize the motive for their existence. How and why would these traits perpetuate over thousands of years or even longer timespans?

Personality Disorders: Usually, these traits become problematic because they are left unchecked, so they manifest too strongly, creating problems. We are not proposing here that anyone should try to worsen these attributes. This list is for understanding and dealing with what you have, what you were born with, or what you've taken from the environment you were raised in.

Cluster A

Short Take: As we observe on The Map, this cluster concerns the northern region. This cluster targets the two types of mind: logical and fluid. For them, these minds are dominant or partially dominant in their inner world, making it difficult to relate to others.

Paranoid
Map: Up North (+ Bottom South through vertical curvature)
Root: The logical mind, Element 6.
Description: Very suspicious of others, unable to trust others without a logical reason. They make up reasons about other people's intentions.
Pros: A healthy dose of paranoia makes us double-check our actions or plans. Suspiciousness, care, and meticulousness are a few qualities of this trait. A person who tilts towards paranoia can spot evil where others don't.
Cons: Evil or harmful intentions can be wrongly estimated. This is the quintessential problem with paranoid personality disorder. The only way to overcome this is to gather more data that can be tested and verified by yourself or others around you.

Schizoid
Map: North
Root: The logical mind + the fluid mind, Elements 6+5.
Description: Uninterested in forming close relationships, for these relationships might interfere with one's life. They can be perceived as distant.
Pros: People with this personality type are very adept at being alone. Because both the logical and fluid mind are involved, they can spend countless hours thinking about and imagining things. They can also act as a pair of eyes outside society, seeing and observing issues with their mechanisms from a different outsider's view.
Cons: Hard to fit in. Their inner experience with their minds rarely fully maps out well with the rest of the world. They tend to prefer being alone and avoid trying to fit in willingly. The way to overcome this is through understanding society. Finding your place in the world entitles understanding the world enough.

Schizotypal
Map: Mid-North
Root: The fluid mind, Element 5.
Description: Odd, eccentric beliefs. Difficulty in forming close relationships because of their differences.
Pros: Spirituality-oriented people are eccentric in their beliefs. These types will always have a new spiritual and unique story to tell. This personality type matches well with the past prophets, people with visions, or intense revelatory experiences concerning a higher power.
Cons: Weird, impractical, and tempted to throw logic into the garbage can. The only way to quench these possible exaggerated manifestations is to ask ourselves what the functionality of our beliefs is, precisely, one by one, understanding how they work and what we can do with them for ourselves and the world.

Cluster B

Short Take: Cluster B is about extreme emotion, from love to pride.

Antisocial
Map: Far East
Root: Extreme Yang emotions, Element 3.
Description: Impulsive, reckless, they don't think about how their actions affect others. Frustrated, aggressive, and prone to violence. Low on empathy.
Pros: The main advantage of this trait is fearlessness. This fearlessness is especially applicable to being ourselves in society. This type of person can stand up for themselves, being assertive and action-oriented. We could also see this trait as combative.
Cons: They are destructive. These types of people are inclined to break things or hurt people. Many people report that without physical training, martial arts, or military training, they would have ended up in prison. The way we generally help mitigate the side effects of this trait is through respect and self-discipline.

Borderline
Map: Far West, Far East (jumps through the vertical curvature)
Root: Extreme Yin-Yang emotions, Element 4<->3.
Description: Coping with strong emotions, mood swings, and complicated feelings. These variations in emotion also can lead to an identity crisis.
Pros: A person who can conjure up a lot of compassion and love can sometimes make friends or enter relationships quickly. From the right side of The Map, they can also switch up to aggression and brutality when they are trembled on. The latter can translate into putting your aggression into resolving things.
Cons: The big con here is relationship instability. It is relatively easy to be careful with our inner state if we see somebody twice per month. However, this lack of frequency is not valid in an intimate relationship. They are prone to either worship or hate their partner. They are prone to this fast inner change of perception. It is not a logical change. Something they like happens, and then a massive wave of love hits them and changes their perception. Sometimes, something they don't like happens, and they become resistant and condescending. We resolve this by having a clear vision of our partner. We don't need to communicate the pros and cons of the relationship. We understand what can be improved and realistically by how much. This way, we can step back and remind ourselves of this

cooler, lower-energy vision when emotions spawn. By doing so, we anchor ourselves so that we don't jump tremendously to the structure's left or right.

Histrionic
Map: (East + West) => Mid
Root: Creativity + High Emotions, Elements 5+4/3.
Description: They like to be the center of attention, overdramatic, and overemotional. They suffer when they are ignored.
Pros: Theatrical, extraverted, entertaining, the life of the party. These people do not pull their punches regarding self-expression in their work and daily lives.
Cons: They tend to exaggerate issues in their lives. You can be theatrical about your enthusiasm, but you can also make a minor issue into a Greek tragedy. Exercises such as meditation and mindfulness are great tools. They work by allowing yourself some inner time to cool off and then express your emotions.

Narcissist
Map: East
Root: Lack of proper Yang emotions Element 3 (negative).
Description: A high sense of self-importance is needed to cover their low self-esteem. They might act towards achieving a goal without considering others.
Pros: A natural leader. By often presenting their achievements, people become aware of their competence. If we take somebody more skillful but without the capacity to boast about their achievement, the latter person will not be seen by the people around, and people will not gravitate towards them.
Cons: Although it might seem that they have high self-esteem or pride, they mostly mimic it. This constant pursuit of showing off or acquiring validation is the essence of negative behavior. It is like a dim light bulb connected to a low-power battery. It is not that the battery is enormous and complete, but that it lacks energy and capacity. A good exercise for this issue is noting our accomplishments and knowledge about the world. An excellent positive sense of pride will arise, and at the same time, we realize that when comparing ourselves with the rest of the world in some areas, we are at the bottom end achievement-wise. By writing down what you know at a high level, you understand where you are compared to others on the scale of knowledge, and again, you observe how many valuable things you don't know. So the solution is honing this sense of pride for your work plus the observation of all the things that you cannot do and never will be.

Clusters C

Short Take: Cluster C lies down to the south, rooted in the instinctual realm. Negative emotions, such as fear and anxiety, characterize it.

Avoidant
Map: South-East
Root: Inhibited pseudo-sexuality, Element 2 (negative).
Description: Fear of being judged negatively, prone to social anxiety. They might want affection but worry they will be criticized and rejected.

Pros: Precocious. Not all social interactions are worth it. There is an array of "must interact with" and an array of "I want to interact." These people are keen on guarding against negative people entering and wasting their lives.

Cons: Social avoidance, lack of social mingling. It's not necessarily that these types do not yearn for social interaction; they are afraid of being shunned. It is not the schizoid type with an endless array of things to think about. We tackle this through two methods: thinking and action. We can use our logic to prepare for the actions ahead in this direction. Think and be honest: If these people would drop from the sky in your lives, how many friends and acquaintances would you like to have, and how often would you like to see them? Now that you have your numbers and vision, the only way to fix it is through action. Action in this case would be exposure, slowly and gradually increasing levels of social exposure.

Dependant

Map: Far South

Root: Basal survival instincts, Element 1 (negative).

Description: They give away accountability for their responsibilities and fear acting alone. Tendency to put their needs last. A fear of being left alone.

Pros: Stability generators. They yearn to connect and stay connected to people that they care about at any cost. They are the last ones ever to abandon a friend or let go of a relationship because of some insignificant issue with said relationship.

Cons: Draining others, lacking autonomy, can become dependent on a negative relationship. We've mentioned not letting go of a relationship for silly reasons, but this can quickly escalate into accepting any negative behavior of the other person so that they are not left alone.

Obsessive Compulsive

Map: South-East

Root: Starts from lack of physical order, instinctual in nature, elevates itself to higher planes, Element 1-> till the 7th.

Description: Think of the title itself: compulsion. "Need to" is rooted in an instinctual call to action for specific reasons. They plan and organize until the last detail. If they can't follow that highly complex plan, if something unexpected comes up, it brings them much anxiety. They tend to have exceptionally high standards for people and themselves.

Pros: Perfectionist, conscientious, and attentive to the project details. They are the type that can draw out a plan and stick with it. Even if that plan takes everything out of them, they will still do it, at least to the best of their ability.

Cons: Rigidity. All things have to be in my control, arranged in the exact way that I want to, and executed in the order I want them to be. This rigidity can become cumbersome in a relationship, making it difficult to merge two lifestyles of two separate people. In its extremes, it can derail us from macro progress, being too focused on small details. This hyperfocus on details can lead to near burnout. It's easier said than done, but the solution is letting go. Let's focus on silly rules first, not the ones that are objectively healthy for you, such as not smoking, not drinking, or taking drugs. Pick one of your self-imposed rules, and let it go for a pre-established time, a day, a week.

Map On: Religion - Mythology

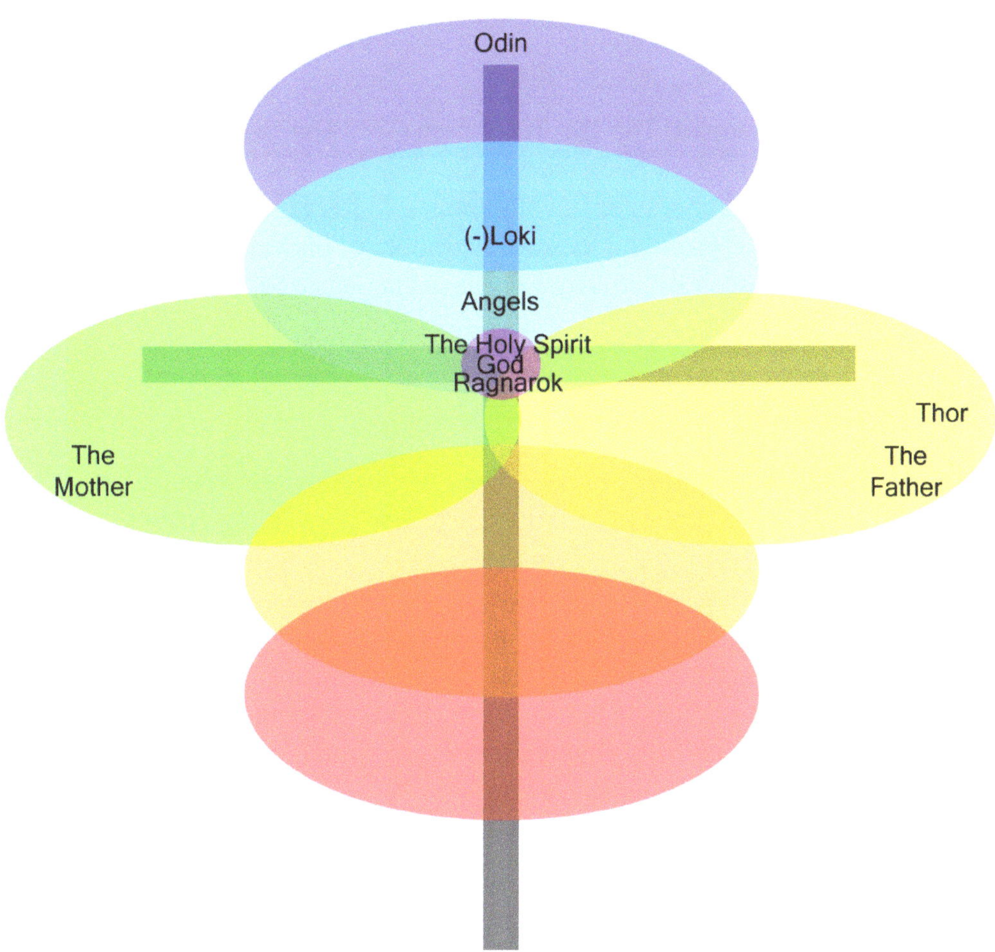

Overview

Disclosure: I was born and still am an Orthodox Christian. The following are my interpretations..

Depth Of Analysis: We are going to discuss just some high-level concepts. We are not going to do a deeper dive. This mapping aims to add even more correlation weight to our map. Seeing that even spiritual/religious concepts find their place in our Map is quite something.

Takeaway: Although the details differ, archetypes arise in similar cross-cultural patterns. In this field, you can find cool videos and learn more about how archetypes are portrayed in various cultures, religions, and mythologies. This points out, yet again, that there is a unifying inner structure at play when thinking about humanity over the millennia. This structure is presented through stories, using expression and emotion, but it can also be analyzed through the logical mind.

Spiritual Experience: The Trinity

There are three fundamental types of spiritual experiences or high-level perceptions. This manifests itself, for example, in Christianity through the Holy Trinity. Multiple interpretations of each of the three extremes exist, and we shall analyze them.

The Father
Position: Middle to the East
Element: 3
Interpretations: Fair Judgement; The Old Testament God; The manifestation of The Wrath of God.
Familial Correlations: The father is easily attributable to the familial father figure.
The Spiritual Experience: Feeling an incredible amount of energy, perceiving God near you, while you attack your objective, invincibility, and indestructibility.

The Son
Position: Middle to the West
Element: 3
Interpretations: As far as I can tell, Jesus's values are archetypal feminine/yin: love, compassion, and forgiveness. So, even though He's 'The Son,' in my opinion, he embodies the opposite archetype.
Familial Correlations: From a familial perspective, I would argue that these values align more closely with the mother, strengthening the familial connection even further.
Note: There is a dichotomy between Jesus and Mother Mary. This correlation is not inscribed in The Trinity aspect. This is a different matter of discussion.
The Spiritual Experience: One with God. One with the planet, nature, humans, the sun, the moon and the stars. Loving and thriving with life.

The Holy Spirit
Position: Middle North
Element: 5
Interpretations: The Holy Spirit is regarded as a messenger, a role also shared by angels in Christianity. We are looking directly at the expression, as in the vocalization of the Divine.
Familial Correlations: This no-filter purity and expression maps very well with the archetype of the child.
The Spiritual Experience: Divine inspiration. Visions, rapidly changing metaphors, ideas, stories, and timelines. The Cosmic Dance. The place of pure play, where nothing is wrong.
Note: Wisdom is a high ideal. If we view wisdom as the application of understanding, it first requires a foundation of understanding. Our logical minds certainly play a crucial role in understanding, but logical understanding is not a spiritual experience, however magnificent it might be.

The Proportions Of The Cross Symbol
The Concrete Aspect: Historically, the cross used in Roman crucifixion was not equilateral. It looks like that because that's how a human body is shaped. There isn't anything more to its proportions at a direct level.

A Fourth Type?: Regarding spiritual experiences, though, the form tells us something. You have these three directions close to the center; the bottom part is far away. If we observe The Map, the seventh element (violet) is closely related to three elements. This fourth element would be the southern region, but it's not directly connected. In other words, there is no instinctually rooted spiritual experience.

No Examples: Even in methods such as Kama Sutra, where they strive towards attaining spiritual experience through intercourse. You can get a higher perception, but it's part of the three that we've already mentioned. You can get one of the following two:

Archetype Yin: In that physical scenario, you can perceive "togetherness" at a couple or cosmic level. Spiritual experiences are rooted in the Yin and west side of the structure. It's not an instinctual reaction in isolation, even though instincts can potentiate our emotions.

Archetype Neutral: It can also go to the top. After the climax moments, sexuality fades away, and there is a sense of floating and freedom. That type is rooted in the Middle-Top spiritual experience.

Norse Mythology Concepts

Odin
Position: North
Elements: 6 & 3
Description: He is also known as "The All Father". He also tends to be portrayed as wise and knowledgeable. He is also the Norse God Of War. In The Tower Chapter, we discussed contrasting colors. This showcases how the contrast works between Yellow (Element 3, fire) and Indigo (Element 6, logic).
Overlap: The Christian Father we've described in the Yellow zone bestowed Judgment fairly and knowledgeably. We've discussed Him in relation to spiritual experience, that being the East side of The Map, but we observe that the 6 & 3 correlation also stands for Him. You need knowledge and understanding to pass fair judgment. Through this deeper analysis and comparison of elements, we can see that Odin and the Christian Father, particularly in the Old Testament, share significant overlaps.

Loki
Position: Middle North
Elements: 5 (negative)
Description: The Trickster, The Liar, The Betrayer, The Backstabber. He is playful but usually in a negative fashion, spreading deceit rather than truth. And what truth he tells, he only tells half of it.
Overlap: The overlap here is with the Holy Spirit as a Messenger. The elements overlap, but one is pure white, positive, and the other is the wholly negative aspect of that element.

Map On: Fantasy!

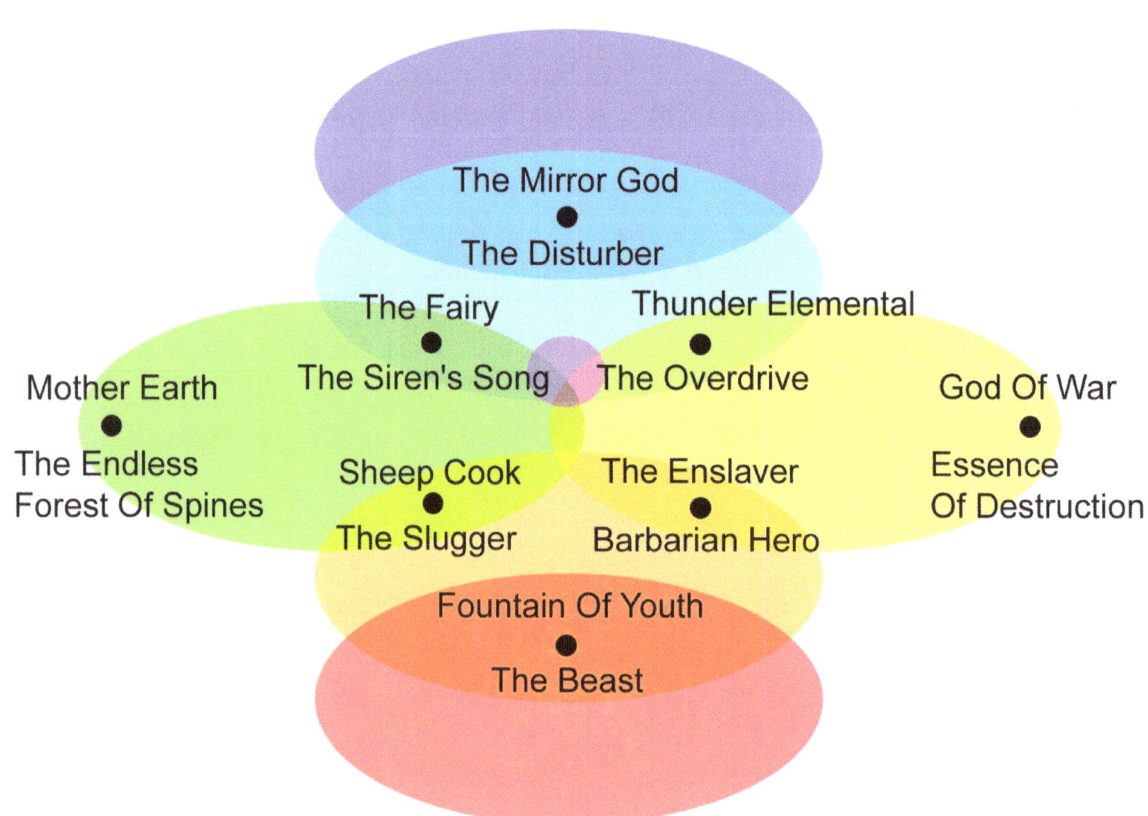

Short Overview: We can easily derive characters from our map. They will be stereotypical of the zone on The Map. We are not creating overly complex characters but creatively portraying what the directions are about. The dot represents the position of the above and under writing.

Positive-First: Characters/Creatures

Archetype: North
Name: The Mirror God
Elements: 6+5
Description: A tall abstract being. It doesn't, per se, have a body. What could be described as its head is a bunch of mirrors pointing to a giant eye.
Role: Each mirror represents religious wisdom, philosophy, scientific observation, psychology, and common sense. They all converge into the central Eye of understanding. This Great Eye symbolizes knowledge of the vastness of the human experience.
Positive Traits: Holistic understanding. Observing that what brings us together is more significant than what pulls us apart.

Negative Traits: Too much focus on what overlaps regarding these facets may lead people to forget the roots of each side of understanding, eventually leading to the crumbling of the facet itself.

Archetype: North-East
Name: Thunder Elemental
Elements: 5+3
Description: Floating entity made out of a continuous current of thunder. It does not touch the ground, for its root is the sky, ideals.
Role: Bring people in need into an overdriven state so they can proclaim their next large Quest! This Spirit brings us a massive surge of positive energy that we project towards our chosen path. This projection lingers for two or three months. The positive emotional ignition sends us into overdrive, making us capable of envisioning our grandiose goal as doable.
Positive Traits: Initial batch of massive motivation. It helps us set Grand Goals. It makes us feel invincible towards the hardship of Destiny.
Negative Traits: This surge becomes pure delusion if not quenched after the initial batch and taken at face value as a logical truth. This can lead to a misinterpretation of feelings and reality.

Archetype: East
Name: The God Of War
Element: 3 (+7)
Description: A towering figure, a machine of war. It is completely engulfed in armor of steel. Its yellow glowing eyes pierce through every soul that dares to look The God of War into his eyes. It is said that fortune favors the brave. It is said that once you've settled your mind towards a direction, standing toe to toe, facing this God, and proving your fearlessness is the ONE TRUE test of your devotion to your cause.
Role: It is the core of motivation, the spear of strife; it manifests the very essence of progress. It brings to us the inner state of DO or DIE.
Positive Traits: Motivation, active purpose, Quest-like attitude, all-or-nothing attitude, devotion to a deed/cause.
Negative Traits: Element 3 represents fire. This devotion to the cause and Quest-like attitude can and will burn us up if we abuse it. We can get drunk with the power of progress. This can lead us to hindered results because we've spent too much lifeforce in too short of a timespan or are incapable of feeling positive emotion towards our accomplishments.

Archetype: South-East
Name: The Barbarian Hero
Element: 3+2
Description: Taller than most humans, highly muscular, wide-shouldered freak of nature. His long, uncombed hair and beard dance into the wind while training his strikes against a grand old oak. The preferred weapon is dual-wielded one-handed axes. Preferred fighting style, up close and personal. The Barbarian doesn't take any kind of personal insult without a fight, a physical fight.
Role: Besides aiding humanity up close, he is a symbol. He is a symbol of nerve and guts. He reminds you to hold your head high and be indifferent to your social standing. He is a symbol of pride and brutality.

Positive Traits: Stand tall attitude, anti-bullish behavior, pride in being human and doing your best.

Negative Traits: Although some pride is necessary to function correctly and integrate ourselves into the world, it might become too high and too large compared to our deeds and actual accomplishments.

Archetype: South

Name: The Fountain Of Youth

Element: 2+1

Description: A well of nourishment, physical well-being, and longevity. It is imbued both by the forces of earth, part of the reason is dug deep, and by the flowing nature of water.

Role: We were given this fountain to pass on through generations. This fountain reminds us to cherish our lives while accepting life's ever-changing flow. It is provided to us by the ones before us, and we must hand it over when our time draws near.

Positive Traits: Physical health, physical fitness.

Negative Traits: One can become obsessed with one's longevity. People are meant to be born and wither away in the endless circle of Samsara (the Dream of Life). By obsessing over our survival, we might not enjoy life's pleasures. Regarding goals, we might take them on with a handbrake of fear.

Archetype: South-West

Name: The Cozy Sheep Cook

Element: 4+2

Description: We can find this Sheep at every Inn travelers encounter during their journey. By the playful fire, the Sheep is always there to offer a sparkle of pleasure to your taste buds, but the yummy food it cooks.

Role: This sheep loves to offer tasteful pleasure, comfort, and warmth.

Positive Traits: Positive enjoyment of pleasures, comfy clothes, and a nice cup of tea.

Negative Traits: An excess of this energy leads one to become engulfed in comfort and pleasure.

Archetype: West

Name: Mother Earth

Element: 4 (+7)

Description: All-encompassing, a being that our mortal eyes cannot see all at once. It manifests continuous fruitful love and acceptance. It regenerates our bodies and minds; it heals us from our wounds and sorrows.

Role: Holder and breeder of life. The essence of togetherness, the womb of acceptance.

Positive Traits: Love, recovery, acceptance.

Negative Traits: After we've recovered, it's time to go; it's time to move. This type of energy can lead us to want excess emotional comfort over progress.

Archetype: North-West

Name: The Fairy

Elements: 5+4

Description: Cute, winged, playful, childlike, giggling spirit of the forest.

Role: Bringing peaceful optimism to humans. The Fairy is, most of the time, a symbol of an untroubled, peaceful time ahead of us. It reminds us that life is a game and we need not stress out. It stands as a connection to our inner child.

Positive Traits: Chill, calmness, serenity, optimism.

Negative Traits: An excess of this energy can result in a lack of seriousness about our goals and may hinder progress. It can also make us not want to grow up into our adult selves, making us dream about the tranquility of the past.

Negative-First: Characters/Creatures

Archetype: North

Name: The Disturber

Elements: 6+5

Description: A tall, skinny being with a large head. It has a multitude of eyes, each pointing in a different direction.

Role: Convincing humankind that different ways of observing the human experience are isolated and discriminate between themselves. Be it religious wisdom, philosophy, scientific observation, psychology, or common sense. All have different truths, and there is no unifying element to gather them around, only the madness of the void, which all shall succumb to.

Negative Traits: Confusion, creating isolated clusters that do not meet and handshake. Fake smiles and insincere handshakes.

Positive Traits: As much as all these ways of seeing human existence point to one source of truth, the human experience in itself, it is true that each way of seeing it brings its discriminate differences to the table.

North-East

Name: The Overdrive

Element: 5+3

Description: A bird-like massive being with a thousand heads. Each head shouts a different story, a different song, another correlation.

Role: Unlike The Disturber, this creature fares far from logical assumptions and philosophical directions. Its effect on feeble minds is like a thunderstorm within a thunderstorm, with feelings of excitement towards fleeting directions, each thunder representing random bursts of excitement and their immediate disappearance.

Negative Traits: Uncontrollable, chaotic excitement. Rapid inner change of our inner storyline.

Positive Traits: If our own story is crystalized in a way that doesn't make sense to our inner self, then chaos is necessary to disrupt the flow and re-generate a story, a metaphorical song that will be in line with our being.

Archetype: East

Name: Essence Of Destruction

Element: 3 (+7)

Description: The closest description would be the explosion of a star. A massively violent gargantuan manifestation. Its form is the very splitting of atoms.

Role: It evokes in humans a genocidal thirst for destruction, along with every subset of this type of energy. It does not care about your place of birth, your age, or your eye color. It does not care about your ideals or your ability to aid it. It only conceives of the rubble that will stand behind it after it has imposed its will.

Negative Traits: Mindless, disregarding any type of instinctual safety.

Positive Traits: The Essence of Destruction doesn't lie. It doesn't pull strings, it doesn't manipulate. Its hate is pure. It will tell you its intention, and you shall pray that it doesn't manifest its wrath towards you.

Archetype: South-East
Name: The Enslaver
Elements: 3+2
Description: This character class not only wishes to dominate but gets a kick out of it. They want to make people bow down to their wishes to be superior in the hierarchy without proving themselves worthy.
Role: Breeds desire for power for power's sake. Not highly manipulative but rather bully-ish energy of supremacy and dominance. A tribalistic approach to dominance.
Negative Traits: Subjugation, stomping on people's necks, shouting louder than the other.
Positive Traits: Sometimes, you have to fight fire with fire. The most logical and knowledgeable person does not always win a debate. We must be able to grow teeth and show them to the opposition if peaceful conversation is thrown out the window and the matter at hand is essential.

Archetype: South
Name: The Beast
Elements: 2+1
Description: It always lingers in the dark and chooses caves as its layer. The Beast can take many forms, mostly told through tales, as no man has ever seen it in clear light. It most likely has many heads, each representing a different creature.
Role: Lust, greed, fear, and terror are its meat. With every excess humanity does, the beast grows stronger. Every time such energy is expelled from our behaviors, the beast makes its presence felt, sucking the life energy out of us.
Negative Traits: Hyper-hedonic behavior. Instinct first, irrational acts generated by terror.
Positive Traits: Although The Beast, left unchecked, wreaks havoc, it is also an essential aspect of being human. We are not floating angels singing songs to God all day long. We need to integrate these animalistic aspects harmoniously.

Archetype: South-West
Name: The Slugger
Elements: 4+2
Description: A disgusting, filthy, slug-like being. It roams slowly the bogged forests, spreading its life-draining mucus wherever it's crawling sickening carcass.
Role: Any creature, humans especially, see how horrid this creature is from the outside. The catch is how the beast feeds when its prey gets stuck in its secretions. There, an inviting sense of calm and warmth is generated in the victim. A desire to sleep, a willingness to let go slowly. The sensation is so addictive that the victim, instead of fleeing, gets drawn deeper into the secretion.
Negative Traits: Hyper-comfort seeking, being sluggish, moving very slowly, heaviness, indulgence in disgusting eating habits.
Positive Traits: An amount of relaxation and a treat here and there are fine. With zero of this manifestation, the human experience would be arid, and the world would suffer burnout after burnout.

Archetype: West
Name: The Endless Forest Of Spines
Elements: 4
Description: It is a dimension of its own, a vast, foggy, soul-tearing forest of sunless dawns.
Role: It brings the torment of the human condition, a hurtful reminder of the frailty of life.
Negative Traits: Pain, hurt, loss, grief.
Positive Traits: Loss and grief are natural parts of life. We hurt as we go through them. After we go past them, they are reminders to call a loved one and be there for somebody, for life is frail.

Archetype: North-West
Name: The Siren's Song
Elements: 5+4
Description: A consciousness-piercing song that breaks us from reality and makes us drift towards nothingness. It mangles the mind into detaching itself from reality—a dream without substance.
Role: It attracts people into a dream-like trance. It makes them forget about their duties and their mission. The Siren will continue singing, stopping only when you've realized you've grown old and have nothing to show for and nobody near you. That's its biggest treat, looking you into your confused eyes as your dreamy delusion becomes horrid understanding.
Negative Traits: Forgetful serenity, delusion of happiness, isolation in dreams.
Positive Traits: Sometimes, we need to escape reality for a while. That's why we watch action movies, sci-fi, and fantasy movies. We all need a break from the weight of the world.

Map On: Metal Songs Clusters

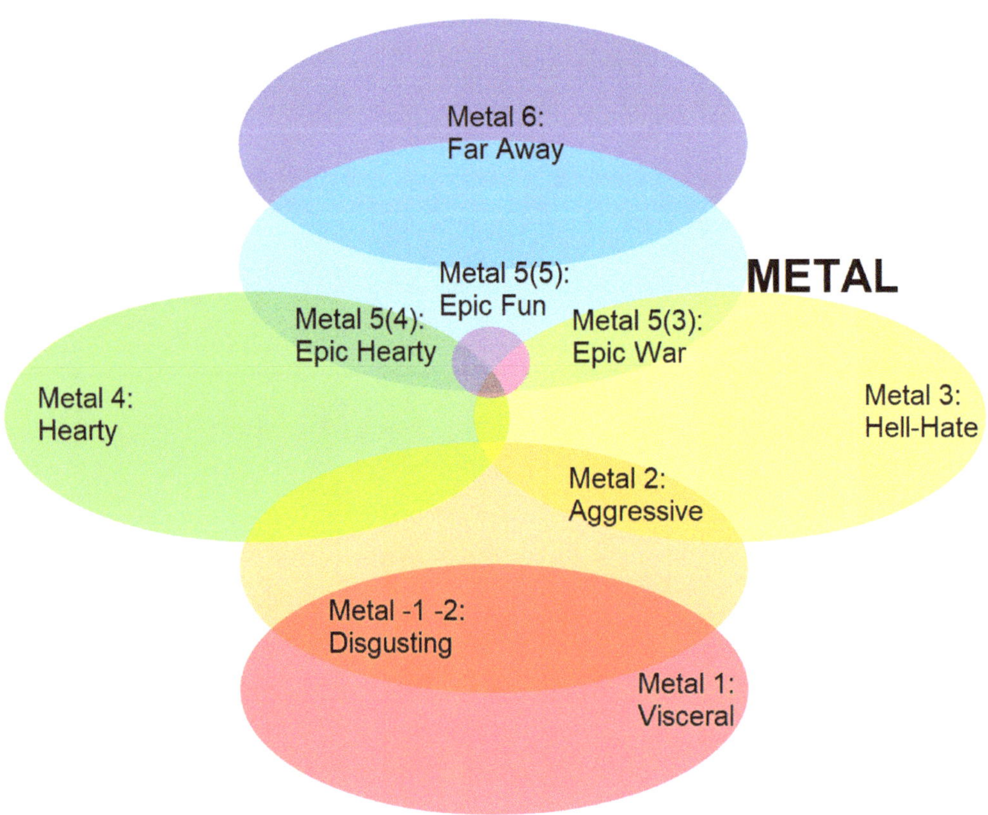

Overview

Music as a Tool: Music has a root in the 5th Element. Considering this element as a gate of expression, any type of human experience can be expressed through "it." "It" is a very abstract concept regarding the inner world. Of course, you have instruments, vocalists, and lyrics, but music as an abstract concept related to the inner world is formless; it can become anything.

Let's Have Some Fun: Our structure is a serious construct. Let's take a more light-hearted approach to understanding ourselves. In the metal scene, there are always discussions about which band fits the exact sub-genre. We will use our map to define clusters based not necessarily on genre/sub-genre but on what those types of songs activate within us.

Generally Applicable: The fundamental idea of analyzing songs based on how they interact with our inner world is a general concept. It can be applied to any type of song or parts of songs, snippets, if you will.

Metal Music

Type Of Examples: Note that most song examples are regarded as "extreme metal," so they won't be to everyone's liking. I will not list a thousand songs here; I will give several examples that nail the cluster best from the music I know. Examples are formatted as [band: song]

Initial Root: Elements 5+3. Metal music is a form of self-expression, like it or not, a form of art. So, we have Element: 5 at play here. But with what type of emotion is the creative gate combined? Well, with the aggressive, destructive nature of our feelings, Element: 3, be it good or bad.

Root & Other Clusters: Besides the root of the genre, music can overlap with other points on The Map. We will take the original root and mention the different clusters in place.

Lyrics: They also have their place in these categorizations. Most likely, lyrics must be searched for because of the distorted nature of metal vocalization. It's okay if you don't get the lyrics, but look them up if you want more context.

Clusters

The numbers generally point to The Tower. If the complexity of the numbered presentation is higher than the base elements alone, explanations will occur.

Metal -1 -2: Disgusting
Vibe: Decay, putrefaction, disintegration, futility of biological life.
Functionality: Sometimes, we are disgusted with ourselves, with the world. The sun is shining, and the birds are chirping. Our inner state is not correlated with what's around us. It's like life is laughing straight to your face in regard to your position in it. Something like this works positively because for X amount of minutes, while listening to songs like this, we feel that what's inside us is congruent with what is on the outside. This breeds acceptance, we feel understood, and those negative feelings wither away step by step.
Examples:
- Cattle Decapitation: Not Suitable for Life
- Acrania: Disillusion in a Discordant System
- Analepsy: Colossal Human Consumption

Metal 1: Visceral
Vibe: Huge amounts of caffeine, speed (as a drug) sensation. It makes you want to clench your teeth and sprint quickly.
Functionality: These songs are good for "bringing us from the dead." They click with our basal instincts and activate them. Note that if you genuinely don't have energy left, they don't work. They work with untapped energy levels and bring them into the foreground.
Examples:
- Siberian Meat Grinder: For the Cult
- Awakening Sun: Void Silence
- Slayer: Repentless

Metal 2: Aggressive
Vibe: In your face, guts, mano a mano. Animalistic confidence and steadfastness.
Functionality: Sometimes, we need an ego boost or a confidence boost. This type of music is designed to appropriately increase your ego levels so you can tackle your daily life with the efficiency you deserve.
Examples:
- Five Fingers Death Punch: The Way of the Fist
- Hatebreed: Facing What Consumes You
- Korn: Right Now

Metal 3: Hell-Hate
Vibe: This type of energy is reserved for tasks or things. I've had enough; I will completely and fundamentally obliterate my goal. I am Fire, I am Death.
Functionality: Hating the wall between you and your goal, not people or groups of people. This hate can lead to a massive surge of energy and lift the restrictions placed on our minds.
Band Examples: Ov Sulfur, Immortal Disfigurement
Examples:
- Slaughter To Prevail: VIKING
- Mental Cruelty: King Ov Fire
- Paleface Swiss: The Orphan

Metal 4: Hearty
Vibe: Here, we have metal combined with sadness, love, loss, and grief.
Functionality: The metal side of things acts as a shield so that overwhelming Yin emotions do not encompass us. This type of metal acts as a bridge between our repressed Yin emotions and their inner manifestation.
Examples:
- Killswitch Engage: The Fire
- Heidevolk: A Wolf in My Heart
- Heaven Shall Burn: The Sorrows of Victory

Metal 5(3): Epic War
Vibe: A new Quest! A new Journey! Excitement combined with intensity at its max. Shouting in pouring rain while thunder fills the skies and thunderclaps ROAR.
Functionality: This type of music helps us potentiate the excitement we get from completing goals. It's a celebratory type of music. Interestingly enough, it mimics some functionality that alcohol has when we want to celebrate a conquest.
Band Examples: Sabaton
Examples:
- Amon Amarth: Deceiver of the Gods
- Powerwolf: Christ & Combat
- Gloryhammer: The Unicorn Invasion of Dundee

Metal 5(4): Epic Hearty

Vibe: It is metal, so it's still rooted in the northeastern part of the structure. These songs make you want to draw a tear while looking up at the sky. Optimism, idealism with a warm fuzz added to it.

Functionality: These songs are helpful when we need to feel that West/Yin emotion. The combination of metal and this specified emotion makes it so that they are easier to feel, deal with, and experiment with. Part of the emotional range makes you feel powerful, the metal aspect, while the other softer side can manifest also. When we can't fully experience that Yin emotion, this type of music acts as a bridge. The air element, element five being doubled down, these hearty emotions will also tend to be more towards their positive side.

Examples:
- Feuerschwanz: Warriors of the World
- Little V.: Dark Souls 3 Theme
- Enterprise Earth: Psalm of Agony

Metal 5(5): Epic Fun

Vibe: Stupid, dumb, fun. Party music with funny lyrics.

Functionality: Playfulness, laughter, decoupling from seriousness.

Band Examples: Alestorm, Romahoy, Korpiklaani

Examples:
- Electric Callboy: Tekkno Train
- NanowaR of Steel: Valhalleluja
- Brave the Sea: Old Maui

Metal 6: Far Away

Vibe: Letting oneself go into the cold void. Low emotion, low base. Bleakness, black and white.

Functionality: These kinds of songs work well for detaching ourselves entirely from the world. Another effect they can have is a closeness to nature. Nature, not as your meadow or field of flowers but somewhere far into the mountains, surrounded by mist. This kind of music can also bring us a cold, fresh calmness. We perceive the experience as fresh because the instinctual side is pretty much not stimulated, but the mental elements within us are. As a technical analysis, these songs also resemble white noise.

Examples:
- Darkthrone: Tansivlanian Hunger
- Azaghal: Nemesis
- Durbatuluk: Der Quell

Metal 7-0: Hazy

Vibe: If at least 2-3 styles occur closely simultaneously, we could consider this category "Hazy." Of course, we could generate sub-sub-categories and be even more specific. For me and for what I was listening to at the time, this level of specificity was sufficient.

Functionality: When you just want to listen to something, but not anything specific, more like background noise that you don't actively pay attention to, with no clear, distinct vibe or message.

Examples:
- Mick Gordon: Rip & Tear
- Shadow of Intent: The Heretic Prevails
- Whitechapel: The Saw Is The Law

Metal 7-1: Complex

Vibe: This is where you have two distinct aspects (clusters) playing with each other. They can be in a continuous stream together, but you can hear and discern these two vibes. It might also come as periods of aspect A and then aspect B, where they are separate.

Functionality: Depending on the clusters mixed, you could be looking at any of the above categories. These types of songs are varied and musically interesting, particularly in the transition and blend between styles. Many songs have some of this variety, but these showcase it extremely.

Examples:
- Lorna Shore: Into the Earth
- Nachtblut: Meine Grausamkeit kennt keine Grenzen
- Synestia: I, The Devourer

Getting Back Into The World

Introspection Benchmarks

The Introspective Situation

Reasoning about these inner issues won't solve the external issues affecting us. This type of Quest will solve open wounds from our past that haunt us, even at the unconscious level. This type of Quest is not one of pleasure but of need. It is not 'fun' or 'nice'. It is an Epic Storm of Light and Shadow, psychological chaos and madness at its best. It is a symphony of Glory and Horror.

Precision: When is enough, well… Enough? How can we figure out when we are reaching the end of our need for such introspection? Clearly defining these limits is so that we don't spiral endlessly without purpose, but be clear and concise. Concise, such as a sniper rifle, not a sawed-off shotgun, in our introspection and inner journey.

Finale: Going inside and figuring out the root of our inner states and unfortunate inner issues is beneficial. This type of Journey is advantageous to an extent. We need to return to earth after we've ventured through our minds. As in the Hero's Journey, we must return to "the village" and "back home" and bring back what we've learned. We could also see this Journey as the great Serpent from the Norse mythology Oroboros, in the sense that the snake exists at an initially small scale; after it has grown up, it will surround the earth and bite its tail, finishing its cycle.

What Is A Quest?: At a high level, a Quest is a deliberate direction we strive towards. At a lower, more specific level, a Quest is a primary target or goal for a given time. It's the thing that, when you have time and energy, you pour every internal resource towards it. It can span through months or even years.

Introspection Quest Dangers: It would be good to have a handbrake when starting an introspection quest, especially if a lot of work is done in a relatively short time. When do we pull said handbrake, and why? Deep introspection usually involves doing few practical things, especially when you are in thinking and imagination mode. It is not ideal to be in this mode for years. We need to clarify and define what we are searching for and how we can test this amount of knowledge gained.

Introspection About: The Past

General Question: Does something from the past upset you enough?

Type Of Influence - Acute: Acute is akin to a trigger, a specific scenario where your inner world breaks and crumbles. Acute triggers are sometimes obvious and easily observable from the inside and outside.

Here are some examples:
- Short, very intense periods of unrest, agitation, and anxiety.
- Exaggerated bursts of anger.
- General rapid shifts to any part of The Map, sometimes when it wasn't the case to get there internally.

Type Of Influence - Chronic: A chronic effect would reflect on our inner state for long periods. It is more difficult to perceive the chronic implications, for we can adapt around them and treat them as "our normal selves." For these categories, examples would be in the range of:
- Repetitive, intrusive thoughts about the same subjects.
- A sensation of something holding you back from manifesting your better self.
- Something keeps you from enjoying your life.
- A looming sense of doom.
- Experiencing an inner void, deep sadness without current outer reasons.

The Human Condition: Nobody is perfect, and no ideal brain exists. Parts of these influences and sensations will more or less exist anyway. That is why it is essential to subjectively determine how much we can tolerate these manifestations so we can live our lives positively. There is no one answer.

Solutions For Atypical Scenarios: Besides the sorrows of being alive, we have solvable problems, problems that aren't in the typical spectrum of the human condition but atypical, outside of our norm. Envision an inner world where these matters are solved enough. Knowing from the get-go that the heavier the inner issue is, the greater the benefits of trying to solve it will be. Knowing, especially if that influence was present your whole adult life, that there are some parts of your mind that you can't even conceive of being OK. The deeper the darkness, the brighter the light at the end of the tunnel.

Introspection About: The Prezent

General Question: Is the world clear enough to you?

Understanding Ourselves: Understanding that we possess various facets, aspects, and ways of being brings serenity and allows us to integrate all parts of ourselves. These can be high mental idealistic aspects or our profound unconscious instinctual nature. There shouldn't be any significant unclarity about our impulses, urges, wishes, dreams, or preferences.

Understanding People Around You: Ideally, we should have enough understanding of the fundamentals of the inner world, personalities, and traits so that we can understand our close environmental interactions. Regarding our evolution of experience, the closer the people are, the more valuable it is to understand them at a fundamental level. As a general ranking system, we could look at the following:
+ **Family:** Intimate Relationship, Kid(s), Parents.
+ **Friends:** Close Friends, Lighter Friends.
+ **People You Know:** Buddies, Acquaintances, Social Circle.
+ **Macro:** The general movements and directions of the world.

Understanding People Around Quantity: A thousand hours of understanding X acquaintance will weigh less than putting effort into understanding, say, your father, child, or partner. The amount of experience required is subjective. At least at a high level, you understand, not just accept, why people are the way they are around you. The closer they are, the more you'll get out of this understanding.

Benefits Of Understanding People: The purpose of this understanding is the reduction of negative emotions. When you at least generally understand why everybody does what they do, you won't feel the need to judge or belittle people. This understanding eventually brings peace and makes your inner and outer life more bearable. Another benefit, especially if your inner construction is rare worldwide, is that you can pinpoint what you want from human interaction moving forward. In other words, finding where you genuinely fit in is vastly more accessible.

Understanding Your Interests: Generally speaking, the more interests you have, the more structure and clarity you need. Even though you are not necessarily an expert on one of your interests, at least having a structure of the knowledge you brought into your mind is beneficial. It reduces chaos.

Interests - Tool For Clarification: We've talked about how the logical mind is the main element that controls ego, pride. Having a short hierarchical structure of everything you know and are interested in clears up your current position of knowledge of the world. It is more straightforward than it seems. Just write a list of your interests, then, in a nested fashion, add sub-chapters, sub-sub-chapters, sub-sub-sub-chapters, and so on, with short descriptions at the edges of the "sub-..." parts.

Understanding - General Knowledge: There is a timeline, a series of events that have brought you all the possibilities and tools you have at hand today. Whether it's reading this book, holding the physical print, or using the gadget you're reading it on. The very fact that you know how to read. We need at least a basic understanding of how and why we have ended up in our current geopolitical and industrial positions. You don't need to be an expert or be weekly up to date about events, but if the current state of the world, in the general point where you stand, seems nonsensical and brings distress, then a little more knowledge and understanding would be ideal.

General Knowledge - As A Thing?: This interest falls into the category of things because although people are obviously in the midst of it, you don't know or interact with them. You are looking at history and facts that do not directly surround you, and you have almost no power or influence regarding them, so it's a colder view and a more faraway understanding. General knowledge also builds a timeline of humanity, a timeline which is a thing, not a person.

Introspection About: The Future

General Question: Do you have a plan?

Direction: Based on everything you understand about your past till the present, what would the direction or the next direction be? Having a direction in mind based on what you know about yourself, how you work, and how you function is essential. Why this is for you and maybe for others isn't. Be specific about why the other directions aren't for you. These other directions might be very similar to the direction you choose, and without clarity, there will always be that "what if?" voice in your head.

Plan - Steps: Have clear steps to be taken for a year. This allows you to configure load and deload periods in advance. Plan 3-month blocks, where the last week or two is either a vacation or your workload gets reduced by half or more, depending on the type of effort. Thinking like this allows us to track progress. Seeing this progress clearly, we will have a better image of ourselves. Even if we fail for several days to do what we set out to do, we will see our progress as a block, which allows us to see the overarching progress.

Plan - Epochs: This is high-level stuff. That stereotypical place where you see yourselves in 5 years. This depends very much on your age. If you're 35 with two kids and a steady career, it is easier to see five years from now where you are heading. It is more difficult if you're 18 and barely starting college because more opportunities and variables are at play. Do your best to sketch out a five-year direction. These five years will be delimited by epochs of 1 year.

Advancements In Planning: Don't put a lot of pressure on yourself if it's your first time or one of your first times writing a plan for several years. As you advance through life, your planning improves, and you become more confident of the path. Being more certain of the path, you can "see in the future" for longer. In more advanced planning stages, you might even be able to plan for 20 years or have some constants you know that must exist your whole life.

Scales Of Success: As humans, we have varying energy levels. In a higher state of energy, we are more optimistic about the outcome or see ourselves putting more effort into making the outcome greater. In lower states, we look into the future with, well, not pessimism, but with a cautious eye, and we also account for change or events that are not in our control.

Moderating The Extremes: You have two extreme estimates at the ends of these visions. Cut the very edges of the extremes from your written plan. So, the ends could be ultra-optimistic and outstandingly pessimistic. For your optimistic vision, include some daydreaming about how the outcome could be possible and how that would play out. For your cautious estimate, focus on the minimum amount of success you would be content with. What could I live with, and how could I ensure a minimal state of success? The optimistic version will bring us more positive energy to our vision, whilst the minimal success part will help us reduce negative emotion about said direction.

Abstract Direction: All the logical processing mentioned above still applies. We can also use an abstract dream, such as an inner ideal, to focus on. For example, we might want to gift our efforts to somebody's self-growth, or we could want to experience more self-expression and creativity. The abstract dream might encompass a lot of intensity as an emotion. This category is last in this chapter because, without a concrete direction, this daydreaming becomes, in time, more of a curse than a gift. It's a call to something that seems unachievable. <u>We can</u>, through logical structures and analysis, figure out how to apply this abstract inner call to our direction in life. Let's just not forget amidst all this reasoning, that it all started from a vision, a dream.

Overthinking

Preface: I propose a different definition of overthinking. My definition stems from pragmatism: "Does it work?" Thinking a lot about something is not necessarily overthinking. "Over" entitles too much, but what is too much, and how can we reason about the quantity that makes it too much?

Negative Loops: If we think about that mistake, that negative encounter, that shortcoming of ours, our processing sounds like this:
Bad Event -> Replay -> Magnify It -> Replay -> Magnify It -> Replay -> Magnify It
From a psychological perspective, that would be called an anxiety loop. This loop is pointed and tends to spiral down. It has no positive functionality; unfortunately, it's the type of thinking that's just harmful.

Useless Loops: Consider thinking about a trivial matter or a plan of moderate importance already well-established. Then we continue to reimagine the same steps or trivial approaches. This loop type is not inherently wrong, but when repeated a hundred times, it outputs the exact same results every time. It's stagnant and a waste of time.

Positive Loops: Thinking about a Grander Meaning, a Grander Direction, or focusing on a mantra (a set of short statements that shift your inner state to a better place) breeds positive energy. If we loop over this situation 100 times, our faith, mood, or whatever we need more of, will more or less significantly increase. The law of diminishing returns will mean that our positive loops decrease efficiency if we repeat them one after the other. It will diminish so much that if overused, it will become a useless loop.

New Loop Angles: This is the "money maker." We not only think but also rethink a complex situation through <u>a different prism</u>. For example, if we are thinking about something regarding an unclear human interaction from the past, we could conjure up various systems and prisms of viewing the human experience, such as The Big 5, The Dark Tetrad, The ABC Clusters, The Tower, The Map, etcetera and so forth.

New Loop Subtleties: This works great if the subject at hand is very important. These could be simple differences in our inner state when we think about the situation to paint a holistic representation. Looking at a problem from a more action, pragmatic inner state, a more agreeable/disagreeable state or idealistic state, will create new points of viewing the same situation. These new points and new angles yield a more robust, genuine understanding.

Useless &/ New: The bottleneck of this new angle situation is the number of systems we have understood until then and our innate understanding of the world. Changing our inner state is difficult, so we might need several days to check out the same problem from different states. We will have useless loops in the mix until we figure out where to get another angle. If our thinking doesn't get us new data for a prolonged time, then it's overthinking. If that happens, we need to focus on getting ourselves in a different inner state while thinking about the problem or use/learn a different prism to look at the situation.

Re-Entering: Abstract Focus

Defining The Enemy

Ideology: This is akin to integrating our "dark selves" or "Id." Where "Id" means our darker selves, Ego means our usual selves and Super Ego is the highly idealistic version of ourselves.

The Way Of Defining The Enemy: This is an abstract concept. It works best when we use our fluid mind trait. Metaphorical enemies can also be defined more logically, but as observed in The Map, the peak of logic, the north, is far from emotion. If we characterize this enemy purely by logic, it won't target our deeper selves, so it will be superficial.

Peak Of Re-Entering: We are returning to the world and moving. That entitles the strife half of our inner world. The peak, as discussed in The Map of the inner world, is aggression. But aggression and its evil cousin, hate, must be directed at lifeless targets. The direction should be towards abstract concepts, not towards your fellow human being. That being said, how could we define this abstract enemy?

Starting From Concrete Situations

Your enemy can be poverty, that would translate to:
- House for the homeless
- Nutrition for the starving

The positive will to help in these sectors abstractly converts into selflessness. What about the enemy? In our example, greed might be involved. So, you could imagine the enemy as a bloated organism that hoards resources to become larger. To give a title to this creature's curse: The Bloat of The Hoarder's Greed. From this description, we can create specific and personal depictions and namings of the create itself.

Starting From An Abstract Concept

Your enemy can be unclarity, in the form of:
- Lack of organized data.

The enemy here could be described as a Disturber. This abstract creature will divide the objective complexity of the truth into tiny, minute, isolated factions of knowledge. Eyes can be used to represent points of view. These creatures will have many unorganized eyes without a clear focus. Flight can also be used to describe the type of creature. As the saying goes, a creature that flies is not attached to the ground and can have 'an eagle's view' of a situation. In our case, the creature has this upper view but purposely acts to disturb The Map that it sees.

Re-Entering: Strategies

The 100 Reasons Strategy: Wait, what, 100? Yes. When we have a goal in mind, we usually narrow our focus on the most critical aspects of our motivation. We draw strength from a few reasons to move forward. While that is the basic mechanism of direction, we can enhance it by acknowledging the variety and multitude of aspects that drive us forward. Give yourself time and attempt to write down 100 reasons why you want to pursue this goal of utmost importance. Realistically, you won't be able to generate 100 reasons. But we are forcing our minds to open to new angles from which we can pull motivation. All these angles of motivation increase our sense of meaning regarding our chosen direction. Study the 'The Tower' chapter for inspiration. Here is a possible example.

Multitude Of Reasons: "I want to work towards and succeed at this goal because:"
- I want an extra source of income
- I want more action in my life
- I want to prove to myself that I am capable of materializing results
- The way my life is set, it tends to make me too relaxed, so I want something to keep me tense enough so that I don't become a blob of laziness
- I want to prove to myself that I can stand on my own two feet
- I am going to do it just for the sake of striving
- I want to show the world the fire that I keep locked inside
- I want to have fun; I want that fun to have a meaning and direction to it
- I want to express my opinions
- I want to interact with people that are similar to myself
- I want to have problems to resolve, things to think about
- I want to increase my capacity for reasoning
- I want to have a Quest till the Day I Die

As we can observe in this example, it is not about trying to reach that absurdity of 100 reasons. It is about deep diving into ourselves and pushing ourselves to the limits of our self-understanding and imagination.

Re-Enter - Tall Strategy: This is great for situations where a clear evil in our life keeps us from becoming what we could become. This is focusing oneself on the peak, the most crucial aspect of your re-entering. Pick the most significant bottleneck of your life and make it a mandatory task to work on, activating a tunnel vision mindset. A vision where nothing else that you're engaging with matters now, just that one thing. Usually, one finds that practical things make you 'move' back into the world. Of course, the past is settled enough, the world around you is clear enough, and the vision is clear enough, but how do you start? We shall analyze that in the next chapter.

Concrete Pathways

Concrete Way: We've resolved our past issues (enough), the surrounding reality is clear (enough), and the future vision is strong (enough). Now, we need a step-by-step strategy to shift from introspection to returning to the world and being present in our lives. Not all life changes are created equal, some having higher weights than others. We will present a priority list and explain the reason behind them.

From Disaster To Safety: No matter how heavy the toll of the introspection was, we will take it step by step. We shall build or rebuild the base through progressive overload. After we feel the ground under our feet stable again, we can work towards our higher goals.

Alcohol/Drug Consumption

The Tower: Element 1 (negative), a rotting root

Alcohol
Cease alcohol/drug consumption: We first have to target the worst of the worst. This doesn't need to be a lifelong change/choice. We take a pre-planned period, say six weeks, to establish this as a steel rule.
Alcohol & Hormones: Alcohol messes up negatively with our hormones. A better hormonal balance will result in a higher drive to work on the following stages of the pyramid.
Alcohol & Gut Bacteria: As weird as it sounds, there is a correlation between the health of our gut microbiome and our mental state.

Weed
Low Energy: The calming effect doesn't exist just in the night we use; it also reflects on at least half of the next day.
Food Cravings: It is far more challenging to attempt a balanced diet in either of its three forms: hypo/maintenance/gain phase while we smoke or have this substance in our system.

Alcohol & Drugs - Dopamine: Dopamine is tightly intertwined with reward. We can reward our brain for an action that doesn't lead to something better. The pitfall of this is that we will be less likely to yearn for activities that naturally produce this neurotransmitter. We are being falsely satiated and satisfied with our lives without the improvement we would gather.

Reasoning: We start with this step so that we don't try to reach our higher goals chained by the negative implications of substance abuse.

Basic Activity

First, we've concentrated on stopping our roots from rotting. Now, it's time to add more activity to our lives step by step to realize our end goals.

Survival: Do ok at your job, so much so nobody is complaining with good reason about you. If you are passionate about that job, you will elevate the attention and energy given towards this direction. In both scenarios, we need to start small but significant enough not to go downhill. So the first task is to do OK.

General Movement: We are starting small, so we will walk around the block, not ordering food but getting up and buying it. From a horrible shape, any amount counts at this level. We will not be able to run a marathon just out of this, but we are slowly building back our base to prepare for grander goals and results.

Regiment of Maintenance: We are discussing building a weekly routine that achieves simple parameters. Orderly house, clean enough environment, clothes washed, adequate personal hygiene, bills paid, and having reasonable healthy food in the house for several days. We do not stray from the minimum. Remember, we are building a base. Having these resolved for weeks on end will lower our anxiety levels because the unconscious won't feel in danger, threatened that our basal needs are not in order.

Food

Junk Food: Multiple aspects of nutrition can mess up our progress. The most obvious is ultra-processed foods. As a general rule of thumb, think of them as those types of foods that you cannot make at home. These are usually in the middle of the supermarket. The amount is also essential here. If everything nutrition-wise is dialed in for 75%+ of your caloric intake, then you can add some non-ideal sources of calories to that remaining 25%.

Glucose Crashes: Sugar in itself is not 'evil'. Macro-nutrient-wise, fruits are made out of sugar. We experience a damaging glucose crash when we eat enormous amounts of carbohydrates in a single sitting. PS: We do not have a daily "required" amount of carbohydrates as we do for protein or fats.

Lack Of Protein: If we eat inadequate amounts of protein, our body tends to signal it to use through hunger. Unfortunately, this hunger is a general feeling, with slight variations of sensations in regards to macronutrient needs. So, if we tend to be overweight, eating too little protein will make us crave calories first with a subtlety only of protein craving. The recommended grams of protein for physically trained people, training which you should be doing, is about 1.6-2g/kg.

Lack Of Fat: Usually, people over consume saturated fat. People on hard diets tend to forget the necessity of adding fats in their weight loss diet. These two categories of people suffer from the same nutritional deficiency: monounsaturated and polyunsaturated fats. With these types of fats added to our diet, we would have a minimum requirement of about 0.6g+/kg of fats per day.

Fruits and Vegetables: We should have some in our diet unless we have a specific intolerance or immune response to them. They aid not only at a gut level, but different micronutrients, such as vitamins, minerals and flavonoids, have their roles.

Tastefulness: On a fat-loss diet, we want to avoid hyper-delicious foods. These types of foods can be ultra-processed, and we also should take into account dishes that are extremely flavorful. The issue with these is that we just want more of that food, making it challenging to maintain our caloric deficit. In the opposite situation, if we want to gain weight, we opt for more flavorful dishes while still ideally avoiding junk food.

Lesser Addictions

Short Overview: This is not to say that these don't have measurable side effects, but realistically, they are way less than the categories above. This category is less imperative, so we can draw some intermediary steps that, in time, sediment. Once we have a solid foundation, we can introduce more challenges to further our evolution.

The Tower: Element 2 (negative), excessive pleasures

Dopamine 2.0: Porn/smoking(tobacco)/junk food are not at the level of drug/alcohol abuse. In these directions, indulging in them, especially excesses, will numb our brains. This numbness leads to satisfaction. This heightened artificial satisfaction will lead us to do less positive activity, for we are already rewarded for our minimal efforts.

Porn Addiction

Sexuality & Motivation: Especially for young people, porn is disruptive. Our motivation to do well in life also has a direct sexual connotation or at least a pseudo-sexual connotation. If we disregard and couldn't care less about "our force of attraction," we won't have the full spectrum of reasons to be successful in our hands. Porn falsely satisfies our brains, making us think that, on the plane of attraction and sexuality, we are at the top of our game.

Masturbation Is Ok: We are not targeting "no fap" behavior. That could be excessive and either make us obsessed with sex or inhibit our sexuality altogether. But there are points to be made about capping on sexual activity, especially the type that you do alone.

Intermediary steps:
- Hardcore -> softcore (porn)
- Reducing the frequency of using porn
- Masturbation without porn
- The masturbation frequency cap depends on the following:
    - If we are in an intimate relationship or not
    - If the sexual desire level is too high, we can get obsessed with sexual thoughts. Then, the cap might be too rigid.

Smoking Cigarettes

Realizing what cigarettes do is essential. There is that dopamine response, which is the overarching theme of this subchapter, but there are more factors at play.

Calming Effect: Smoking also calms us down. We take deeper breaths, do repetitive movements, and don't feel socially awkward for standing outside doing nothing.

Mental Activation: Smoking tobacco increases your focus by employing epinephrine. This increase in focus also comes with an increase in tension, so there's a tradeoff.

Directions: We either try to quit smoking + nicotine or smoking in itself. Vaping is not a suitable replacement, so we won't be concerned about that.

Intermediary steps smoking:
- Add nicotine supplements
    - Patches, gum, pouches
- Reduce the number of cigarettes
- Delete the usage of cigarettes
    - You might need more nicotine from alternative sources

Intermediary steps nicotine:
- Write down the amount of nicotine consumed
- Every other week, cap it lower

Layering Our Goals

Basal Restrictions Example: In this example, we are targeting six weeks. The idea is that not all restrictions and life changes are created equally. We are still good if we can't hold until Layer 3 and manage just until Layer 2. If we keep the restraints until Level 3 and drink on one weekend of the six weeks, it will create a domino effect that messes up the layers above, too.
Layer 0: No alcohol or drugs. Even if I do poorly at work, whatever happens, I abide by this rule, dot.
Layer 1: Basic physical activity, reasonable work performance, house reasonably in order, minimal physical muscle training.
Layer 2: I am going to train with moderate intensity. I am not going to smoke cigarettes, but I'm going to use nicotine pouches. I am not watching porn.
Layer 3: For example, if we are single without any kind of partner, I will cap my sexual activity to once or twice per week. More specific food restrictions.

Extra Activity Example: Set up three layers of expectations for each week. These can be extended further, but as you recover and get better at life, these layers can shift. We will take writing a book as an example.
Layer 0: In the beginning, do whatever you can. Even if it's 10 or 20 minutes of your goal. Expectations close to zero at the very inception.
Layer 1: Even if unexpected events happen, even if I feel low, even if I'm spent, this is the steel floor from which I do not stray. For example, 1 page of writing every other day.
Layer 2: We don't feel at the edge; we maybe even feel slightly bored. In this case, it is worth targeting more extra work, for example, writing 2-3 pages every other day.
Layer 3: We feel "the thunder." We are pissed, we want to see progress happen NOW, and we have the energy to back it up, for example, writing every day at least 2-3+ pages.

Physical Training

We should be mindful of our general fitness. Being in decent shape works wonders for our self-image and capacity to work towards our goals. We will focus on beginners' gains to around an intermediate level of training and results. We will outline the basic mechanics and focus on our minimum required training to achieve a mid-intermediate level.

Structure

Frequency Of Training: 2-4 times per week is sufficient for the targeted fitness levels. The lower end, two sessions, would include more compound movements. The four-day split can be focused on either compound movements or specific muscle isolation exercises.

Training Split: We will outline some versions through this prism and rank them by difficulty and expected results.
- A / B, twice weekly training => half body on A day, the other on B-day.
- A&B, twice per week training => entire body twice per week.
- A / B, four times per week => A,B,_,A,B,_,_, where_ is a non-training day.
- AB1 / AB2, three times per week => AB1,_,AB2,_,AB1_,_ => AB2,_AB1_AB2_,_.
  - Where A: deltoids, arms, forearms, chest.
  - Where B1: (can be) back.
  - Where B2: (can be) legs.

Intensity: Intensity in physical training is most easily measured using reps in reserve (RIR).
+ We want to train hard enough to have a stimulus. Our training sets should have around 3-1 reps in reserve.
+ We can also train to failure, even if our lives depended on it when we couldn't do another correctly executed repetition.
- We can also add sets beyond failure when we can complete just half the lift, but this is not mandatory and, at most, a tool for variation.

It's not always about how 'hard' you can work; instead, showing up, doing a good enough job, and having enough meaningful volume will get you the desired results.

Volume: For our targeting an intermediate level, we are looking at about 10-20 sets per week for each muscle group. We are looking at 5-10 sets per muscle group for the minimal required stimulus for growth. A number of 3-5 difficult sets can be enough for muscle maintenance. Keep in mind that compound movements work for the secondary muscle groups. For example, a pull-up set can mean x1 back set and x0.75 of a bicep set. The same goes for push-ups, where the chest is the primary muscle group, and the front shoulder and triceps act as secondary movers. This is how we think about those recommended numbers per set.

Starting Volume: When we begin or restart our training, we could start as low as 3-5 sets per week and then advance in volume as we get more accustomed to it. We don't need to demolish ourselves, especially in the early stages. We need to show up and slowly progress to our target volume.

Execution

Tempo: Tempo refers to the speed of movement in any particular direction, either during contraction or muscle lengthening. These phases are also called concentric (contraction) and eccentric (lengthening). The consensus is that for hypertrophy, using good technique, we want a fast concentric contraction, and for lowering/lengthening, we want the movement to last around 3-5 seconds.

Range Of Motion: The easiest way to describe proper ROM (range of motion) is to do the entire length of the exercise. If we control the weight in the eccentric portion and practice good technique in our warmups and working sets, there is no reason to fear the entire movement. The bottom third/half is significant for hypertrophy. Even if it's the scarier and more difficult part of the movement, know that it brings results (better than peak contraction, for example). In other words, emphasize the stretch. This type of full ROM training is good for our joint's health, but keep in mind that you must warm up, keep the technique straight, and be aware of your tempo. If you're untrained or de-trained, don't jump on heavy full ROM movements. Keep the ROM under control and with a higher rep range, say 10-12+.

Warmup: We don't need cardio for an excellent muscle-building warmup. If we wish to start with some cardio, anywhere from 5 to 10 minutes until we break a sweat is more than enough. If we return from an injury or have a problematic joint, we can specifically target that area before the exercise warmup. The warmup that we are generally focusing on is the exercise warmup. The exercise warmups maintain the tempo and execution form.
  - **First Warmup:** If you are training with weights, go for a weight that you could do over 20 reps and do ten good for and tempo reps. If you're training with bodyweight, start with an assisted or easier variation of the exercise, then move on to the version you'll use for your working sets.
  - **Second Warmup:** Take a weight with which you could do ten reps and five. This is the same idea as the above regarding bodyweight training.
  - **Third Warmup:** Do 1-2 reps with the working set weight. This gets the nervous system jacked and ready for the working set. This set is not for warming up the muscles but for the nervous system for that specific exercise.

Rep Range: Hypertrophy, or muscle growth, can be targeted at a rep range of 5 to 30 reps. We can play around and see what works best for us. We can also change our target rep range after two months, for example, to diversify our training, make progress, and have fun along the way.

Rest Time: The rest time we mention is between sets of the same exercise. For the best results in hypertrophy, we are looking at about 1-2 minutes. The more extended rest periods are generally for compound movements or big muscle groups such as the back or legs. For warmups, we can target lower rest periods, such as 30 seconds to 1 minute.

Progression

Progressive Overload: In time, we want to grow stronger to facilitate hypertrophy. We can do more reps in the same set, especially the first set. Or we can add weight to the exercises in small increments. But how does 10kg X 12 reps compare to 12kg X 8 reps? Some online calculators help you calculate what you could maximally lift by the weight and number of reps that you can manage. Search for 1RM calculators to gauge your progress. It is not an exact science, especially in the high rep ranges, but it can give you an understanding of weights vs. reps.

Calories: To build muscle, we need to be in a caloric surplus of about 300 calories for a sustained period of time, combined with physical training for hypertrophy. For weight loss, we are generally targeting a deficit of about 400-600 calories.
- **If Obese (BMI):** If we can take it, we can increase our caloric deficit. While body fat is high, losing muscle while training and having a caloric deficit is less likely. The leaner we are, the more muscle retention will be affected.
- **Frame:** A 600-calorie deficit will feel in a way for a 120-pound woman and different for a 240-pound man. Adjust as needed.

The caloric splitting can be done in 3-5 meals. Only some meals have to be complete, but it is highly recommended that at least three of those meals contain enough protein.

Deload - Caloric: After 8-12 weeks, we will probably feel "diet fatigue." We will be too mentally blurry and experience exaggerated hunger. We can take 1 to 2 weeks at a maintenance calorie intake. This will prepare us physically and mentally for the next cutting (caloric deficit and fat loss) or bulking stage (caloric surplus and muscle building).

Deload - Training: After 8-12 weeks, or when needed, we can cut our volume by half for a week. This allows our joints to feel good again, and psychological readiness will be high after this break. Depending on how hard you are going, the weight also has to be cut down by 30% to even 50% of your working sets.

Relationships: Proto Processing

Short Overview: The focus here is not relationship advice. This is for people who are not in an intimate relationship or who are close to one. This set of reasoning metrics can help us understand what we are searching for in the first place.

The Setup

Decency & Common Sense: Simple and obvious aspects such as how we take of ourselves physically, groom, and hygiene. Eventually, the other person will see where we live or ask for images, so our place should be decently orderly and clean. We don't need expensive clothes, but we need to pay attention to the fit of the clothes we choose, and of course, they don't get ragged. These are so "in your face" aspects that we usually never think about them, but seeing them in black and white is good. Recognizing the importance of these factors will help us realize that we don't need to be Prince Charming or Cinderella; we just need to focus on the basics first.

Stable Base: As discussed in "Chapter: Concrete Pathways," we need to get our lives in order enough. That means that we have a stable base upon which to build. Sometimes, "life happens" during our existence, but sometimes, "you happens." We want to mitigate the latter as much as possible, where our behavior is not actively bringing us down. This mention is essential because we can project that some sort of a relationship would make us behave vastly differently, solving all our problems, which isn't the case. The base alone won't cut it; we must also embrace individuality.

Constructed Individuality: "Magic comes from within" is an actual phenomenon. First, we need a good relationship with ourselves. We cannot expect God, The Universe, to just spawn an external element that will bring us joy in the long term. After our base is established, we can add exciting activities to the basic functionality of our lives. This is where "magic comes from within" really kicks in. Whether we are single or in a relationship, there is a mystery, a fascination, and a positive way forward for us. This is an advantage, a twofold advantage. For once, we feel independent, and we are not blaming others for our sh*tty lives. Secondly, this is an attractive feature. Even if the person that we are eventually choosing to be in a relationship doesn't have the same interests, these interests preserve our individuality. This existence of individuality potentiates the moments where two become one, more metaphorically or concretely. This works by the means of contrast.

The Search

We would be disadvantaged if we did not make an active effort to figure out what we want in a relationship. Our default vision will likely not match the reality of what we want and need. We will outline some fundamentals to analyze and help us throughout our journey.

Personality Type: We've discussed personality in detail in The Map chapter. Understanding ourselves first is imperative; otherwise, how can we know whether we're a good fit?

Low Resolution: People tend to be too specific about the traits they want to see in the other person. In our analysis, we are being very specific and logical, but relationships don't work that way. We should draw some general, lower-resolution guidelines for what we seek in a relationship.

Prioritization: It is also important to determine which are traits essential to you and which traits you can ignore or overcome. After prioritizing your low-resolution list, you will discover that just a few personality aspects will be fundamental to you. You will also realize that you are malleable, accepting that some less desirable traits might not bother you as much.

A "Good Person": Returning to The Map, the left/West/Yin is where relationships usually work. The peak of this Yin side is the heart, love, compassion, and emotional understanding. As a general rule of thumb, this trait is highly desirable. So keep that in mind in the way you present yourself and act. Nobody says you should be fake about it; just focus, remember that you have that soft side, and manifest it. Also, you can gauge and observe if the other person manifests this trait.

Faking Good: In some cases, the other person creates a false facade to mimic this sought-after trait. Pay attention to minor oversights when the other person talks about their interaction with others.

Rejection: Remember that, just because somebody is "you type" personality wise, that doesn't mean you are their type. Maybe what we've mentioned above is on point, but you are not the type of person they are searching for. The takeaway from this is that: don't try to change yourself into something you are not because of rejection caused by mistype.

Concrete Elements

We should not judge individuals by these metrics, but the crude reality is that they play a role in forming relationships. A positive integration here would be an acceptance of our instinctual urges, desires, and needs and not being ashamed of them. At the same time, we should prioritize what we've previously mentioned about how the person behaves toward us and others around them.

Social Standing: We can look forward to many social hierarchies and try to climb. This also can show more than meets the eye. What social standing? A doctor, a lawyer? The aforementioned come packaged with 'I believe official and serious structures are very relevant,' so at least partly a more conservative thinker. Is that person highly regarded or aspires to be in an artistic endeavor? That shows us other traits, such as creativity and maybe extraversion. Somebody might be a good fighter and have a high social standing, so highly combative and low on neuroticism.

Wealth: Some aspects to consider. Did the person build that wealth or a large part of it? Is most of their wealth inherited? There's nothing wrong with inheriting money, but character shows up with the individual's effort. This does have something to do with their personalities. We are not looking at exact numbers here, but if the person has decent financial capability, it shows conscientiousness. It can also show intellectuality, creativity, extraversion, and neuroticism based on their work field or how they obtained their monetary gains. So even if it looks superficial, there is something more profound to learn about that person based on their work than the material reality.

Genetic Looks: We are looking at the physical traits the general population finds attractive: a person with a symmetric face and height, a man with broad shoulders and a chiseled jawline, and a woman's bust and hip width.

Looks & Presentation: Body morphology is a cumulation of choice over time. Besides being more or less attractive, it also conveys some information about that person's lifestyle and a little bit about their personality. We are looking at this category as a package because different body types (morphology, hair type, hairstyle, etc.) mix well with certain clothes. How the person mixes their body type with their presentation also gives us a small insight into their personalities.

Rejection: Remember that, just because somebody is "you type" physically or presentation wise, that doesn't mean you are their type. Of course, in this more pragmatic category, there are things we can upgrade and improve. These would fall quickly in the category of presentation and body morphology, while wealth and social standing take much longer to improve.

Practical Philosophy

Cognitive Structuring For Introspection

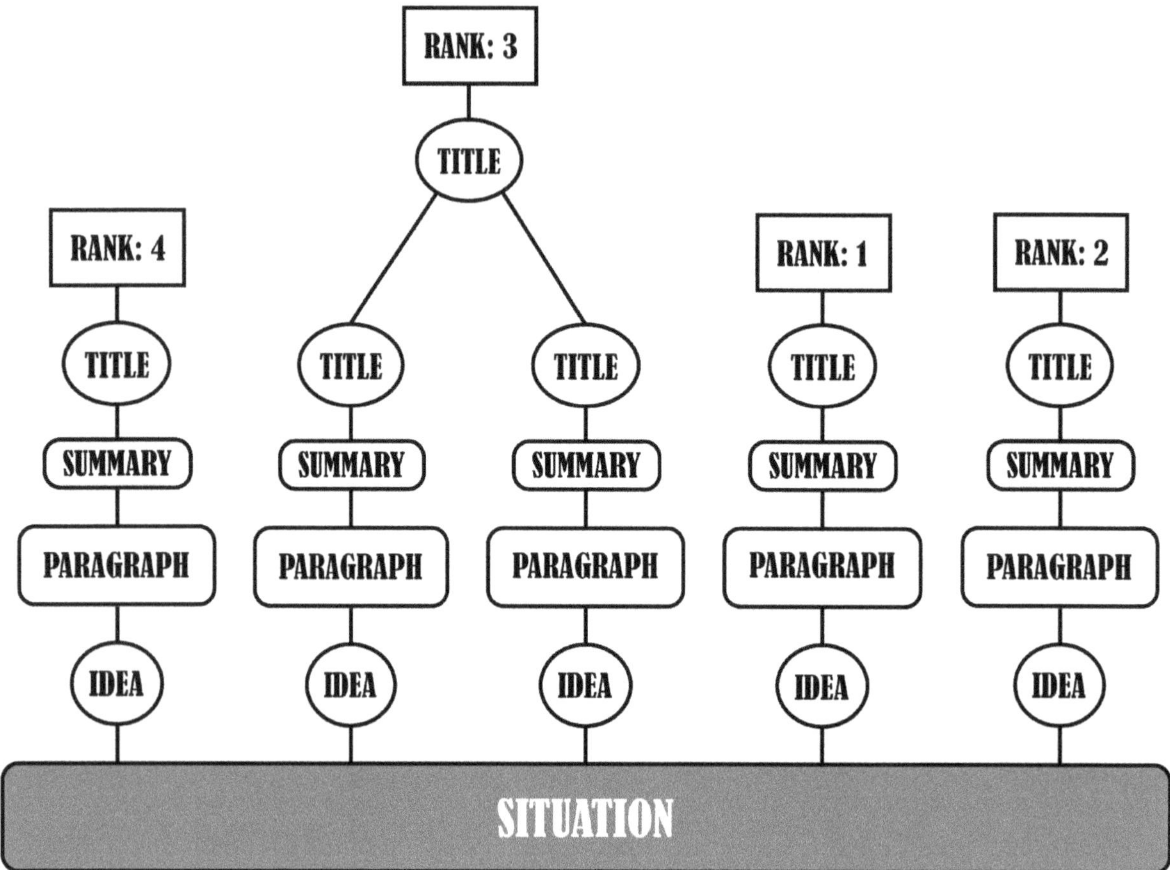

Mechanism

First, let's discuss the basic mechanics of inner understanding. We have a phenomenon of expansion and then one of contraction.

Expansion:
+ **Initial Data:** This is where we lay down every piece of the puzzle relevant to our introspection on any subject related to the inner world.
+ **Unravelling Data:** Through long-form writing or by daydreaming about ideas, we expand these initial pieces of data.

Contraction:
+ **Summarisation:** This is where we take our long-formatted ideas and condense them into a medium-length format. We keep the main essential ideas, scratch unnecessary detailing, and write down our understanding.
+ **Clusterization:** A medium-length format can be 'baptized' by a title. This concoction serves as the title of our cluster, which references the medium-length and long formats of that particular aspect of our situation.

+ **Co-Clustering:** Some clusters are massively different from others; they can stand independently. But given a pretty specific inner situation, it is likely that some clusters that we've written out can be bunched up together to form an even higher-level one.

Presented Tool: Our presented framework will contain the following steps:
- Defining our <u>Situation</u>
- <u>Long Form</u> presentation
- Main <u>Ideas</u> that stem from the larger pool of data
- <u>Paragraphs</u> that describe well enough the root of the situation
- <u>Sentences</u> that bring the description into a more insular level of specificity
- <u>Titles</u> that serve as landmarks, direct references to the clusters created
- <u>Co-clusters</u> which are meant to group out similar enough categories/clusters
- <u>Prioritization</u> as a means to figure out what factors are most important/relevant

Cognitive Structuring Tool: We are going to get very pragmatic, as pragmatic as introspection gets. Long-format writing alone is not enough when dealing with a situation we genuinely can't compute using our working memory alone. If we just use the long form, we are not tapping into the contraction aspect of understanding, missing the points made in our writing. We will outline a step-by-step guide on how to write for introspection effectively.

Roots

Situation: This is a more straightforward step. We write it down, not just imagine it. We write the problem at hand. This situation is the entity in our lives that we cannot compute by using our working memory alone because there are too many aspects and details to compute. By writing things down, at a later stage, we will be able to see hierarchies of importance.

Long Form: This will be done by both writing and thinking. Anything from intrusive thoughts regarding the manner that lingers or pops up to hopes and dreams about the situation's outcome. We are unzipping what we believe, feel, and know about the subject. Even though this alone cannot bring us a resolution, we first need to unravel high-resolution details without drawing any conclusions. Take your time. Either focus more on imagining and thinking or on writing down every bit that comes to mind about the subject. When you feel that you have enough, go to the next step.

Ideas: We can also think of these as roots/factors of the situation. Every idea here is a good idea. That idea might have just a 5% weight in the matter, but it's not 0. If it pops up, it has something to do with our understanding. Write these factors down, along with simple ideas and directions. We can also rationalize them as inner or outer factors to focus better.

Example:
Situation: I want to move to Sweden
Outer Factors: The weather is not hot, there are more rainy days, better childcare than in my country, better wages for my job, and people are more emotionally distant than in my culture.
Inner Factors: I want to leave my past behind, have an adventure, prove myself, and push myself.

Clusters

Paragraph: We should start first with the definition of the word paragraph. According to the first definition from Merriam-Webster, a paragraph is: "A subdivision of a written composition that consists of one or more sentences, deals <u>with one point</u> or gives the words of one speaker, and begins on a new, usually indented line." The critical part for us here is the "one point" aspect. For each idea, write 1 paragraph. We might feel that another paragraph should be written. If that is the case, there are two possible directions:

+ Ensure that the first paragraph is satiated.
    + If there is no more 'room' in the first paragraph, use the next pathway
+ Write the second one
    + Remove it out from the initial idea/factor/root
    + Focus and figure out what other singular root idea this second paragraph that we've written has.

Example:
Situation: I want to move to Sweden
Inner Selected Factor: I want to leave my past behind.
Paragraph: I am sick and tired of the same people, the same environment, and the same unmoving rock that is my country and the society surrounding it. I want to shoot for the sky, and I want to be free. I want to live where people care about what's around them and how they present themselves.

Sentence: We can compress our paragraph data even more. The point is the reduction of chaos. We will compress our paragraph into a single sentence. The purpose of this action is to force our minds again to extract the most important parts. For each section, write a one-sentence summary.

Example:
Summarisation: I want to change the fact that my efforts are not appreciated in society.

Titles: These are the direct references to the clusters regarding the matter at hand. This is a combination of both contraction and inner representation. What does this sentence->paragraph->long form text mean to you? We need to baptize each of these written sentences with a title.

Example:
Summarisation: I want to change the fact that my efforts are not appreciated in society.
Cluster: Current Appreciation vs Potential Appreciation

Co-Clusters

There is a high probability that at least some of our clusters will be very close. In a hierarchical sense, this co-cluster is a quasi-umbrella term that we will use to reference the clusters beneath it. We don't have to do more than that; just clusters to co-cluster where it makes sense.

Example:
Cluster 1: Initial Appreciation vs Potential Appreciation
Cluster 2: Initializing Change For Recognition
Co-cluster: Reaching Towards My Potential

Cluster 2:
Inner Factor 2: I want an adventure
Paragraph 2: Change will never occur if I stay where I am. I know that by going on an adventure, I initialize change, at least the part of the change that is in my hands. If I apply myself, I could get the recognition I deserve. Nothing stands between me and what I deserve if I put a high enough goal in motion.
Sentence 2: It is time to leave home figuratively and literally to prove myself.

Example Co-Cluster Explanation: The first cluster was focused more on the societal environment. The character knew that in his country, people didn't appreciate progress enough compared to other countries. The second cluster provides a more individualistic experience. Everything that matters is the character's strife and choice of change, while the outer environment is less important. Both are true subjectively and objectively. The societal climate takes its toll, for better or for worse. At the same time, we are the ones who initialize The Journey into The Unknown. As we can observe, they can be under a higher level concept of attaining one's potential.

Co-Cluster Depth: Sometimes co-clusters can be co-clustered between themselves. You don't have to stop at level 1 of co-clustering if you observe an even deeper correlation. This is not obligatory and varies by factors such as the complexity of the problem and how deeply tied the situation is to relationships with other people.

Example Conclusion: With our example, a person lives in the southeast of Europe. They fantasize about moving to Sweden. Beyond the practical and theoretical advantages of their society, and likely a more financially advantageous position, one may find that the fantasy of moving to the North reflects an inner desire to metaphorically cool down, emotionally speaking. A move toward more serenity, detachment, and milder emotions.

Prioritization

Prioritization Functionality: This will clear your head regarding what is essential in that situation. You might discover, for example, that the type of enthusiasm you were seeking comes from a different area of life, and perhaps you were projecting it onto a certain type of relationship. The structure might reveal, for example, that the inner choice and your actions matter more than the environment. It could also showcase what you need to focus on to get the most out of that situation. These were only examples; there is an unlimited array of possible scenarios and revelations, but this is how you do it.

Ends Of The Tree: The latter step of co-clusterization can lead to two possible outcomes. Either we have a winner overarching theme or multiple relevant aspects, each with various weights of importance.

Overarching Theme: In some scenarios, co-clusterization can run several deep levels. It can go beyond even that. We can find an overarching theme that unifies our situation's roots. If that is the case, that is your answer. That is the solution to your inner turmoil regarding understanding that situation.

List Importance: If the co-clusters don't share an overarching common core, then we prioritize them. Say you have 5 ends of the tree of clusters/co-clusters. Figure out which is more or less important than the others. With the finalized tree, rank the final branches in order of importance.

Possibility Of Re-Looping: If the tree we've built doesn't result in a satisfactory answer, then we must redo the steps while keeping our initial structures. Try and imagine what other possible factors/ideas could be at play. Your work until now, even if it didn't yield the sought-out result, will be helpful. It is much easier to find new ideas when the ones you've already had at hand are well put and in order. The mechanism of how this works is that you've created a low-energy reference, the titles, the clusters. When you run through your complex array of situational factors, and one of the factors stored in a low-energy state pops up, you get over it quickly, freeing up mental energy and capacity to focus where you couldn't before.

Difficulty Is To Be Expected: This is not something that you can do in your head, not something that you can imagine. That's by design; you can't just figure it out on a whim. That's why we break down every aspect, making shortcuts and then connecting the dots so that we can understand the thing.

Avoiding Emotional Overflow: If a paragraph-> summary -> title brings you pain/cringe/sadness, etc, hide it lower in the document while writing down these things. It is much easier to concentrate just on a paragraph and then see the whole picture. Otherwise, the mind wants to jump and reach conclusions too fast, so you don't get enough depth out of that root/Idea. The situation is haunting you; that's why you would use a complicated system like this in the first place. So, if you have multiple paragraphs in your line of sight, the emotions can become overwhelming, and again, the depth of the analysis is hindered.

Conscious-Subconscious-Unconscious

Caveat: The prism we will use will be mind, emotion, and instinct. These will be our conscious-subconscious-unconscious layers. There are multiple ways of analyzing this aspect of the inner world. We could say that these 3 layers are 3 full versions of ourselves, with mind, emotion, and instinct at play. For our purposes here, we will observe them as layers of mind, emotion, and instinct as separate structures. I believe that is a more straightforward approach. "Id, Ego, and Superego" references Freud's work.

The Conscious

Tower Mapping: These main elements make us civilized compared to other animals.
  + Element 6: the logical mind
  + Element 5: the fluid - expressive mind

Cognitive processing: This is the fast-paced part of our mind, not intrinsically deep. It is similar to a CPU at a shallow level; without a context and depth of data, the CPU is just a 0/1 gateway (oversimplified).

Context-based processing: As more data is brought to the cognitive process, a tree of understanding and prioritization forms. Nodes are not just binary but can be linked with multiple nodes. The arrangement of the nodes also results in hierarchies of importance. These phenomena happen constantly, with more focus or less analysis upon each step.

Memory-based processing: As resolving the problem becomes increasingly complex, we slow down our cognitive processing and give memory more energy. Memory convocation itself is costly. In addition, more energy is required to connect the current processing with the late, or more current, memory.

The Great Filter: Knowledge is crucial, but we are reaching for understanding regarding inner resolution. Understanding is the incorporation of our knowledge. The path from the logical mind to the deeper structures is The Great Filter. The Filter exists because we don't want to absorb everything we hear and learn about from the exterior to our deep inner selves. That would leave us open to a massive amount of manipulation. But we must bypass it when trying to edit our deep inner selves. We do such a thing through abstract concepts, stories, emotional connections, and daydreaming. In the next chapter, we shall analyze how our inner layers are structured and how we can access and communicate with our deeper structures.

Expressing the outcome: When it's time to communicate and express our cognitive results, we output conscious and subconscious elements. The deeper layer can be more prominent or suppressed, but they are connected. For the message to be delivered appropriately, we need intonation, pauses, and talk speed, modulated by the fluid mind and emotion.

Gate: Conscious - Subconscious

Tower Mapping:
  + Element 5, the creative/expressive mind
  + 3 & 4: emotions

Through the prism of these consciousness layers, we will find that the conversation between the conscious and subconscious is not that complicated or vague. The challenges appear regarding the depth of the subconscious manifestation.

Tools We Can Use:
  + Confessing: written, spoken or imagined.
  + Art: long-form writing, poetry, drawing, or painting.

Direct Confessing: When we tell somebody, truthfully, how our day, week, month, etc., was. What do we personally feel about the X/Y/Z subject? Even though it can be a superficial exemplification of how we think, we are slowly exiting the purely conscious manifestation of our mind. About the expression Element 5, think of this as being honest.

Metaphorical Expression: When we start using metaphors and creative analogies, we are dropping down into deeper structures. We use metaphors to convey a stronger emotional reality. In contrast, a mere technical description is not powerful enough to convey the emotion behind the statement.

Pure Abstract Expression: At this level, words fall apart. The imagery or phonic sounds generated by our deeper selves cannot be translated 'live' through text. This type of inner expression can be manifested through drawing or music. The usefulness of this layer is that we can show ourselves or the world directly what we are feeling. The reasons for why we feel that way are unclear, especially on the outside, but even to us. We can later translate what that powerful manifestation was, but for now, we have a clear inner definition of the feeling(s) we've experienced.

Gate: Subconscious - Unconscious

Tower Mapping:
  + Elements 1 & 2: instincts

Unconscious Definition: First, we must define this realm to interact with it appropriately. Through this lens, the unconscious contains reactions, instincts, animalistic urges, and physical needs. These elements are unconscious because you cannot "reason" with them. You can create walls, loopholes, and different suppression methods, but not direct reasoning. I would argue that the ID is perfectly defined in this structure. Here lies the realm of instinct, of survival. The stereotypical depiction of "The Fiery Hell" also fits well here.

Connect the Subconscious: How can we interact with the unconscious if it knows no reason and logical tools are, by definition, in the opposite direction? In a single sitting, we need to establish a strong connection with the subconscious. As we've discussed, we can do that through honest writing, poetry, singing, and freestyle drawing. We know the connection is established when we manifest very clear and deep metaphors that describe the inner parts of us that we usually want to hide away and lock up.

Trigger The Unconscious: With the connection established, we use triggers. Remember that the unconscious is instinctual and reactionary in nature. There has to be a subject to react to. If we want to pull out what lies in the unconscious regarding a person after the subconscious connection is made, look at photos of that person or, if that is unavailable, imagination-driven imagery. Just look at the image, physical or imaginary, for a while. Then, continue your chosen path of interacting with the subconscious, of self-expression. The gate is now open, and deep urges or other instinctual sensations from the darkness will begin to emerge from your chosen path of manifestation. They will probably be scary and hard to accept, so expect a bumpy ride.

Possible Issues

Conscious Inner Processing Limitations: The points made in the conscious sub-chapter showcase the theory of why somebody can be a good programmer, mathematician, or physician yet need to gain the proper skill of presenting their knowledge. They use the cognitive processes in their inner world without experimenting, trying to translate the knowledge and understanding through speech. Without any connection to the subconscious, our knowledge cannot become palatable and understandable to others.

Lack Of Subconscious Tools: Confession showcases a high level of why therapy works. It opens up the being so that words can pull emotions out. After said words are spoken, the logical mind can begin to grasp the feelings that were not crystallized. Note that some people have a very high amount of inner self-thought + the ability to act (as in actor). These people can leverage their different minds to conjure up a genuine dialogue between people all by themselves. Metaphorical expression takes things further. Recursive thoughts combined with imagery can be a window toward subconscious emotional desires.

Difficulty Working With The Unconscious: We have minimal control over how this part of us functions. We can learn, integrate, and be at peace with it. Again, this side is one of survival and instincts. If we don't consider our primordial needs, our perception of life will become negative, and because such a deep structure causes it, it will be difficult to patch up and fix in the future. Our holistic perception is affected because, as we learned in The Tower chapter, there is no thought, emotion, or instinct that exists in a void. If our unconscious signals the higher structures and we completely ignore it, it will ripple up into our emotions, thoughts and perceptions.

Mental Effort Management

Mental effort management is necessary to get the most out of your mind. This type of effort overlaps with strength training and fatigue management. The main difference between the two is the duration of the effort and the recovery rates.

Parameters Of Effort: First, we need to understand the base parameters of effort: volume/quantity and intensity/difficulty. With this understanding, we can be more critical or more lenient with our efforts. We will understand that different types of work are not created equal, and we can better gauge our limits.

Volume: We can also call it width, complexity, or quantity. Regarding mental effort, we could take an example where a lot of volume is required, but the difficulty is low. Let's say you administer a meme page, and you know that replying to comments increases engagement without monetary loss. It is a silly page, so the comments and your replies will be short. The concepts you keep in your memory are simple: responding in a light, positive manner or with an emoji. But the volume of replies is very high. You could do this for 8-12 hours per day if necessary.

Intensity: We can call it height, complicated work, or difficulty. An example of complicated work would be a problematic programming issue. You have a task where seven services interact, sometimes asynchronously, and a simple action causes a chain of events that calls upon 20 files to execute your desired outcome. After three days, you've figured out that 1 line of code, or a simple function, was a little off. This type of work is intense. It is very costly because you have to keep in mind more than five concepts simultaneously to make any sense of the domino unraveling before your eyes. It being so difficult, your stamina, in this case, will be low so that you can perform 4-6 hours at a max of this type of effort, and it's mentally equivalent to 12 hours of replying to silly things on your Facebook page.

For Our Introspection: When trying to implement knowledge such as The Tower or The Map, we work both with high volumetric situations and intense work. We are specific in describing our inner world in this book, part by part. This specificity allows us to work with lower difficulty levels, meaning we can pump more bits in our understanding per unit of energy, efficiency. When we look at the low-level, detailed parts, we focus on those microtransactions between the micro universes, which would be The Tower. The higher levels of presentation and bird's eye view contain complicated interactions. When we get to the higher-level concepts of The Map, we already have low-energy references to the detailed Tower.

General Systemic Load 1.0: You can make an equation for the amount of work you do in a week. It will contain the volume, hours of effort. It will also contain modifiers, intensity metrics. For a physical example, 2h*0.5 for walking, 2h*1.25 for weight training. For a mental example 10h*1 for work you are accustomed with, 10*2.5 for very complicated tasks that are new to you. This is a tool which you can use to gauge your effort and your fatigue response.

General Systemic Load 2.0: There are more systemic loads that, especially the high achievers, don't really want to accept or take into account. Loads such as: relationship stress, bad sleep, bad health, the damn weather and other responsibilities or tasks which do not pertain to your work or main objectives. They are many and minute. If you want to take them into account, you could give each day a general rating from either 1-3 or 1-5. This rating is separate and does not include GSL 1.0.

Computers & The Mind

Some excellent analogies can describe how our mind, with its logical aspect, works on multiple levels.

Immediate Memory: This is similar to the CPU Cache. This is the immediate, speedy memory. Write down a list of two-digit numbers. Try to learn them for 30s-60s. Take a 30s-60s pause. Write down what you've remembered. During this break, you will notice that you keep repeating those numbers so you don't forget them. That is the fastest and shortest-lived memory. You can conceive faster exercises such as flashing in 5 seconds an amount of numbers, breaking 5 seconds and then writing them down. The same memory type applies.

Context Memory: This is similar to the RAM on our PCs. It spans from the context of a discussion to the context of one day. You are talking to somebody for an hour, and your responses and how you manifest them are molded by the context, what happened, and how the discussion went. When you wake up in the morning, you remind yourself what needs to be done that day. You are booting up your system and opening the programs to be used and executed that day. Your RAM resets after you sleep, and you must remind yourself what needs to be done the next day.

***Technical Caveat:** We will describe this type of memory and the next by the means of long term storage, SSD/HDD/Tape. Although they have the same functionality, their speeds differ, that is the analogy.

Periodization Memory: This is similar to an SSD. This spans to weeks, say one, till months, say three. In our journey of progression through life, this memory is best used to periodize our efforts. After 8-12 weeks of grinding towards a goal, taking 1-2 weeks of lower-intensity effort, a break, or a partial break is best. This goes with strength training, muscle building, weight loss, dieting, learning, writing, and any type of extra effort that we engage in. With this memory, we are tracking our progress in our work and seeing patterns of improvement over more extended periods. It helps us remind ourselves of our progression through more considerable periods. For example, in those months of work, a weight loss diet is working, and we've lost x amount of fat; we've written 30-60 pages in our book and learned the basics of that programming language.

Epoch Memory: This is similar to an HDD. We are thinking about years at this stage. Note and observe how the memory speed decreases as the time spans grow longer. That is a direct analogy to computers. The wider the timespan, the slower the information comes to mind. This type of memory is beneficial when we need to step back and observe the general direction of our lives. This is the type of memory we are working with when we are trying to make sense of "why did we choose that relationship?", "why did I go to that college?", "why did I switch up my career like that?". If we are confused by our position in life, the information we need is in this memory state. It comes slowly back and is more challenging to track than the faster ones. Keeping a photo album, journal, or something is good for maintaining a high-level overview of our live's epochs.

Archived Memory: This is similar to tape storage, AM for short. This is your childhood or, if you're older, the years you were young(er). This memory is deficient in speed. The timespan is exceptionally long, 5-10-20 years or more. So, recalling something not kept somewhere in the upper layers of memory is hard. This is precisely the type of memory that we are targeting for the Trauma Resolution Chapter: Step 1. Not keeping every memory in the more costly part of our memory is an autonomous brain function. This function exists so that our brains are more efficient; imagine remembering every part of your life, all at once, constantly. Significant changes in our lives are visible in this memory type.

(AM) Inner Resolution: It is not even a matter of progress through life. You will observe multiple characters through this memory lens. The changes are so significant that we almost talk about a different character. We draw some benefits if we keep this side of our memory tidy. One of the benefits is that we remember that life is worth living, it is vibrant, and new opportunities can be created at every stage.

(AM) Inner Integration: We also understand people who are younger than us better. And lastly, we can understand our parents or people about their age better. We initially might not understand them because they were outputting some ideas we weren't in tune with. Moving through life and observing these different characters, we can better distinguish what part of their output/advice is based on their personalities and which parts are general factors of age that we, too, will experience. By understanding the differences, we can better and more accurately project ourselves into the future, being wary of the negatives that will come with age but at the same time realizing and understanding the personality differences and that our future is our own.

How Creativity Works

In this book, we refer to creativity on several occasions as the fluid mind. We use 'fluid mind' when we present it as a processing unit. When we think of symbols, images, and sounds, we cannot speak of this thinking as logical, so we use fluid.

The Chaotic Gate

Creativity is similar to a warp drive. It is an unknowable black box that receives inputs and outputs something new through its chaotic nature. Any creative piece or idea can be traced down to its initial roots: the artist's instincts, emotions, thoughts, perceptions, observations of nature and society, internalized stories, and other creations.

Simple Example: Look at your hand; imagine your fingers are the roots. Creativity is the ability to tangle your fingers in multiple ways. The roots are not original; the re-composition, the combination, and the warping of these elements is creative. So, nothing is new; everything is re-imagined. That imagination is, at least perceptually, infinite.

Historical Examples: In Russian mythology, is there a crocodile-headed god? Is there a bear god around the Nile? Are there many gods where the surrounding nature is arid and desert-like? Do mythologies that have risen from places with vast forests and changing seasons tend to be monotheistic? The answer is no to every one of these questions.

Old References: Our creative mind draws from within and our surroundings to generate new stories. We are unaware of the subtle roots when ingesting art or hearing stories, and we are also unaware of all the roots when we create our art or generate stories. Nonetheless, we could trace every ounce to a clear root with infinite time. The root is either internal or external.

New Origins: With modern hyper creative work, it is much harder to estimate the creation's origins correctly. We are, if we wish, exposed to a massive amount of data and creative manifestation. It's easy, in comparison, to take a look at mythology and trace back fundamental environmental factors, archetypes, and symbols. It's not that the people before weren't creative enough. Biologically, the genetic differences between us and our ancestors since the dawn of civilization have been minimal. It's the comparatively limited number of different experiences they had.

Talent: As In Skill

People colloquially refer to both these aspects as 'Talent.' In its final form, this description is fine when the artist is high in skill and trait creativity. We need to dig a little deeper if we want to know the details to help our kids, friends, and family better understand themselves. We would also like to know these differences to understand our path in life.

Initial Skill: This can be a marker for the maximum height we could realistically reach in that direction. Some people would not match the elites of that type of manifestation, no matter how many hours they put in. We will take drawing as an example. You will have people who can draw well from an early age and people who can't draw well at an early age. This is your out-of-the-box marker toward this skill.

Skill Progression: The start might be deceiving. Skill, unlike creativity as a core personality trait, can be improved. For example:
- You will see an improvement if you put 100 hours into drawing better and more accurate faces.
- Writing down 100 ways of writing the letter A with any creative derivation that still points to its original A form will give you a more extensive database to draw random creative lettering.
- Reading in pairs of words that rhyme over time will help one develop the capacity to freestyle rap.

Just because the skill is not innate, that doesn't mean that it is not worth pursuing. The potential is not apparent unless it is pursued. So, the skill aspect of talent is underlined by work at the end of the day. Out-of-the-box skills are not definitive markers of skill potential by any means.

Potential Estimation: As in sports, some people are more gifted and can excel at their skills more than others. We can make an informed guess about how far we could take this skill we are working on only after we've put enough work into it. We can only compare ourselves to others to grasp our potential capacity and adjust our goals accordingly.

Living Your Creative Life: Remember that just because a creative skill is not and will not be of "production grade quality" doesn't mean it can't be used to make your life more complex and exciting. Not everything you do creatively in the short or long term has to be monetizable; sometimes, it's just about beauty, self-expression, and the experience itself.

Talent: As In Creativity

Creativity As A Static Metric: The base personality trait "creativity" doesn't move around much during our lives. It's there at some X level, and it remains there. The complexity of what we can output can surely be higher. As we age, we collect more inner and complex experiences while observing more in the outer world. With more roots to draw from, we can increase the complexity and depth of our art. As we age, we also become more inhibited, which is a detriment in the creative direction, but that inhibition can be overcome. That doesn't mean that the base genetic manifestation of this trait changes.

Creativity Vs. Skill - Example:
Kid A: Draws something technically impressive for its age. Let's imagine a tree. This manifestation requires skill. In our example, the kid does not have a convoluted story about its art. The kid saw a tree and drew it well. That's it.
Kid B: Sketches some stick figures; two are flying, and one seems to do some magic. Then you ask the kid what the hell is happening in that image. Twenty minutes later, you realize that skill and creativity are different. Each figure has genders, names, and a short backstory, and the comic-like sketch is just a rendered frame of their stories.

Exploratory Phase: The creative-oriented brain requires a more extended period for development and finding one's path. Because of the unknown amount of potential, the creative individual must try out many creative endeavors until one or more manifestations fit in terms of skill.

Multiple Interests: There is also the matter of fascination. The creative mind has a hand to play in this trait of fascination. By being high in fascination, one is interested in many domains or forms of manifestation. Towards the end of the initial exploratory phase, a creative person needs to evaluate all their interests to ensure that the area they choose to focus their efforts on is the best fit for them.

A Downfall Of Creativity: All this takes time, so a downfall of the creative mind is the high amount of energy required to figure out what type of expression is best. Also, the depth of the message behind the art requires experience, which, by its nature, takes time.

Overclocked Creativity

The base doesn't change, but the roots do. We will observe music for now. In our day and age, at least for some jobs, you could listen to music for 5h+ a day. Let's imagine that the skill is already in place. With how many riffs, vocal manifestations, etc., can you come up with if you've listened to 10 bands your whole life? Compare that to listening to 1000 bands. By being exposed to more bands, you will have a conscious and subconscious library, an archive you can draw upon while creating.

Overclock Physical Example: To differentiate between the base attribute that doesn't change and the overclock, we could look at body morphology. You have two genetic clones: one that lived in 500 AD and one that lives today. The one that lives in the past works in the field and has a low-protein diet, while the other is a bodybuilder on steroids and eats massive amounts of muscle-building foods. The root is the same, but one body is overclocked.

The Best Advice You Can Give

The best advice you can hope to give is to your past self. You know the most about your inner world and how it works specifically for you.

Personal Experience: You might say people are unique; why would my experience be relevant? Well, there are personality clusters. For example, you are very open-minded. Some people are more or less open-minded than you, but some are also near where you score on this trait. Clusters also refer to sex, age, education, environment, preferences, etc. We chose the personality side because it's more difficult to pin down and understand.

Example - Abstract Personality: If you are in the 84th percentile on a trait, your experience regarding that trait part of life will be relevant left and right of this number by at least 10 points. In our example, that would mean that people in the 70-90th range will experience similar downfalls and benefits from that trait. Remember that extremes are extreme; the difference between 50->70 is not the difference between 70->90. It's not a straight line; it's more of an exponential curve.

Example - Concrete Personality: I am writing these methods to deal with the inner world. I know from the get-go that most of these methods of understanding won't apply to people who are practical thinkers (the opposite of being open-minded). More pragmatic people don't have the complications of a chaotic mind and usually do not require much added mental structure. The people that read something like this, you, the reader included, score high on the intellectual (complex mind), creative (fluid mind), or both. The practicality gets even more concrete when we present these structure pieces and advice. By knowing my cluster, I can and will adapt the presentation of the product and of myself.

Being Specific: When we give advice, especially to younger people than us, it is good to first present to them where we are coming from. It is critical to point out the context in which we arrived at those conclusions. That way, they can more easily discern if that piece of advice fits them or not. By being aware of what and who we are, we can figure out if telling that piece of advice to that particular person even makes sense from the get-go.

Advice For Your Past Self: Our philosophy is to advise ourselves. We imagine we are our life coach and spiritual master if you will. We imagine that we teleport all we know now to the past. Before we go to the past, we ask questions such as: "What fundamental factors could have changed the course of history in our lives at that moment?". We are not targeting knowing something specific, like a lottery number. We consider what fundamental truths could have swayed us to a better outcome. We then think and prepare our presentation of that truth, we think about what would have perfected our past at that age. Through this experiment, we have become wiser, gaining a better understanding of how and where the advice should be applied to the people in our clusters.

The Past Is Settled Reminder: Note that regret might pop up when thinking like this. Always remember that you, at that age, in this universe with everything you knew and with the best of your intentions, you've chosen to do that thing or series of things. If you were to go again when you were 17 years old, with that same brain and understanding, you would repeatedly pick the same actions. Meditating on these aspects helps us pull the unnecessary negative roots of past regrets that are too old to be even relevant now.

Extreme Centralism

Getting To The Edges: There is always a left and right to an argument. This is most obvious when it comes to human life and human interaction. To get the most out of a subject, it is best to view, observe, and listen to both sides of the argument.

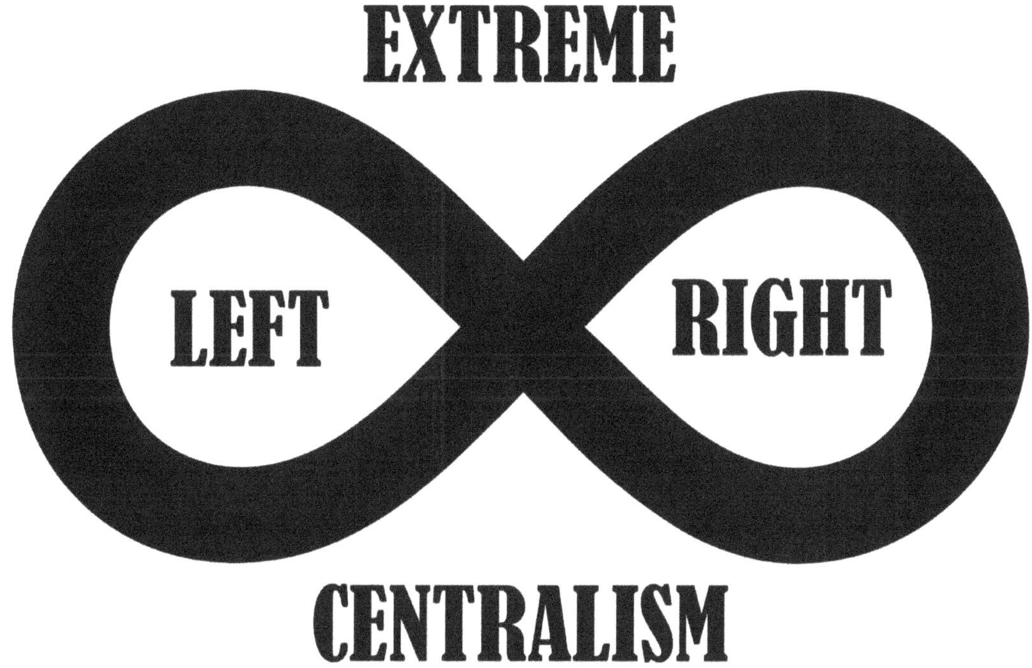

I'm talking about getting even to the edges of the argument on both sides. Writing is an excellent tool for solidifying your understanding of a subject.

How To Write:
- First, write about the camp you are in. Clarify your position on the matter and make an argument for it.
- Second, observe and listen to the other side of the argument. Write down the advantages of that side. You will not be comfortable with the latter. So, you might need a bridge. Imagine what benefits the opposite point of view could have and write that down.
- Third, as you have the positive arguments from the other side, observe and write down the issues with the camp you are in.
- Fourth, write the cons of the opposite side to have the whole picture.

Practical Mind(s) Usage

Pain Point: The trait "Open Mindness," the mental personality trait/aspects, can become impractical quickly. I argue that something should be discarded if it doesn't work practically or well enough.

Practical Spirituality: Spiritual work, customs, and ideas might initially seem impractical, but that's not necessarily true. We need to look at specific examples and categories, not the whole concept. Also, this part of our minds focuses more on grandiose, higher-level results.
Inner Action: Meditating, praying, listening to music, and repeating inner mantras. Here, the question is, does this inner activity shift my inner world in the direction I want it to?
Outer Action: Manifested through rituals, customs, and repetitive actions. There are several good questions for this category. Does the activity change my inner state? Is the activity efficient? Can I change my inner self faster through internal tools?
Categorisations: Clusters of personality, assigned in various manners. Are my categorizations built on experience? Are the categorizations randomly assigned by, for example, date of birth? Are my categorizations based too much on outer appearance?
Inner Belief: Beliefs that cannot be physically tested. Does my belief strongly collide with reality? Does my belief give me purpose and make me a better human? Does said belief(s) randomly throw you off-scent when trying to discern the practical world?

Practical Cognitive: The logical mind can become impractical in inner resolution, change, and progress because it is highly attracted to 'interesting' and detail-oriented. That has excellent benefits, but an individual can quickly become hyper-focused or even obsessed about their plan's details; those parts which bring a 2-5% improvement. At the same time, the individual could have concentrated on the core fundamentals, which bring 30-60%+ to that work and are vital to its operation.
Important Aspect Vs. Detail: In weight loss, the critical aspect is calories in versus calories out. We can become obsessed with more information, such as micronutrients and exact meal timings. In creative manifestation, especially in the internet age, we can become devoured by the precise details of our creative work without focusing on our creation's message and general vibe.
Big Picture: If we find ourselves obsessing over details, here are some questions to be asked to ensure that we exit that mindstate. Is the cognitive processing worth spending in that direction? Is the slight improvement or a little bit of slacking today relevant to the grand scheme? Is it appropriate to focus on minor aspects that give little gain? Maybe we should focus in a completely different direction, such as recovery and enjoyment, which will keep us on the Quest in the long run.

The Two Minds: As we can observe, the cognitive and spiritual, share similar concerns, they can become impractical. The logical mind and the spiritual mind keep each other in check. Think of it as a handshake between The Priest and the General.
Acknowledging Differences: Where The General sees that the Priest's methods work, for some reason that The General doesn't really understand. The Priest, who acts more out of intuition, doesn't understand the necessity of splitting hairs into 14 thousand but understands why that might be the case.
Aware Of The Possible Conflicts: If The Priest gets out of line, the reliance on beliefs and Destiny-Intuition becomes perilous, and control is lost. Similarly, if The General gets out of

line by trying to predict every small step without relying on intuition and experimentation, it too will lead to ruin.

Weird Beliefs

Weird beliefs are constructs of our minds. They have two possible routes of appearing in ourselves.

Receptive-Passive: The passive-receptive one is that we hear and believe a story, from stories we hear as children to doctrine and spiritual stories. These are more like intrusive thoughts; we find that they are there. We can plug them out with effort if that benefits us, but they remain there without intervention.

Active-Generative: The active-generative type of weird belief is the one we create or maintain ourselves. Just because we've heard a concept does not necessarily entitle us to give it thought and energy; that's a choice, a more or less conscious choice. So, we can actively provide power to a weird belief that we passively acquire or create our own based on our perceptions.

Positive Examples

"Humanity Ascending Into Godhood": In the far, far, far future, the chance of this happening is not 0. Maybe, just maybe, there are multiple sequential iterations of the universe, and in this specific one, 'we win' this Great Game. How could such a belief even start to help? It adds, say, 5 points to our hope for the future. The complete opposite would be that humanity would remain more or less the same but with better technology. Our negative attributes will continue to decay the roots of our society, and the end of humankind is unavoidable. Pretty different, right? Even though the first affirmation is relatively insane, it works by giving us a boost of hope!

"Not Even The Gods Knows The Outcome": We might ask ourselves, doesn't some higher being know it all? Isn't our Destiny set in stone that we cannot see? But why would the Gods create us if they knew the outcome already? That sounds boring as hell. What we do with this belief is that we are working with the element of curiosity and excitement. How far can I push myself in that direction? How much can I achieve if I put my weight into it? By believing in such a concept, we elevate our excitement towards the effort and results that will come to a higher, mystical level, which boosts us in our Great Journey.

Some Religious Rules: Respecting some framework of self-restraint is good. Over hundreds of years, people have decided that some sort of structure and lists of behaviors positively influence our lives. We will not go into examples here.

Astrology, A Different Take: If you take the astrological signs and make up a personality cluster system. That might become useful. For some reason, people observed traits clustered in those 12 categories. Not counting at all on the date of birth, but by observing the person, you could say they are "like a Gemini" combined with "a Virgo."

Sign Of The Raven: A more silly one, but an example nonetheless. Say you see a raven, and it starts making its sounds. The raven is a symbol of Odin in Norse mythology. You might internalize that this mystical force of Odin is with you and wants you to know that you are aided in your journey. Is it silly? Yes. Is it weird? Yes. Does it harm anyone? No. Does it make you spend time uselessly? No. Does it give you a boost? Yes.

Negative Examples

Astrology: This is a great example that can go very wrong. You meet a person, you ask, and they tell you the day they were born. You project whatever astrology tells you about that birthdate. It is possible to attribute positives and negatives to that person that are not true. Additionally, you might assign random descriptors to the day you're living in, based on the positions of the planets. By doing so, you might negatively influence your inner state for the day. You might make yourself oblivious to effort management or even the Enjoy/Strife equilibrium.

Overly-Strict Religious Rules About Sexuality: When the rules to be applied become obsessions, they mark our lives negatively. For example, having sexual interactions is a natural need. Hyper rigid rules will likely just cause us frustration and a lousy ID integration. The unconscious needs have to be met to have a fully complete life.

Overly Strict Religious Rules About Nutrition: Another example might be periods of self-restraining nutrition-wise. The knowledge and resources differed when these self-imposed restrictions were a good idea in the form presented in ancient texts. If we follow this belief that XYZ will purify us somehow, we might be missing out on better ideas of cleansing our bodies that are available through modern knowledge. For example, if we are overweight, a keto diet will be far superior to a diet without meat. In our example, we would still benefit from restricting our pleasures but gain something pragmatic, such as weight loss.

Overly Complex Higher Beings: Indeed, the belief in a singular Higher Power or this Power divided into several aspects can be very beneficial psychologically. On a smaller scale, the idea that life and consciousness can differ from the one we humans experience can be an exciting train of thought that can uncover knowledge. But spending countless hours imagining how the 5th dimension connects to the Pleiades and the Martians inside Mars's core is another matter entirely. We might be wasting precious time and effort on something that doesn't bring anything to our lives or those around us. Fantasy and escaping reality to deload our being are one thing, and strong very beliefs and analyses about abstract creatures are another.

Chaos Gets Us All

Don't Amplify Darkness: Ideally, we would add the least amount of extra darkness to our situation in dark times. First, we add negativity to reality by succumbing to our fatalism and nihilism. But these views of the world sometimes just spawn in our minds without much control. In these moments, we need not blame ourselves for our worldview at that moment, which will add even more negative weight.

Finding The Light: Call it "Wrestling With God" or "The Agony of Existence," these realities sometimes show their ugly faces. We must remember that there is no light without darkness because there would be no contrast to realize that light exists. Dark times are given to us so that we find that white dot which provides us with hope. In time and with willing effort, this perception gets increasingly engraved into our perception. Yes, the body breaks away, and the mind slows down, but with a mindful attempt, there is no reason to believe that the times ahead have to be darker than our pasts.

Brain Configuration: Autism

My Experience

In 'old' terminology, the closest description would be Aspergers. Generally speaking, I'm about halfway on the high-functioning spectrum of autism. Inside me, it manifests as:

A. Low innate understanding of human beings
B. High on the ability to see patterns
AB. Higher interest in things rather than people.

Terminology Pet Peeves

Yes, I said high functioning. Yes, I said Aspergers. I know that the terminology "has changed," but it has worsened. The original "high functioning" and "low functioning" aspects of autism are not named perfectly; they could be improved. These two extremes of a "spectrum" are vastly different in manifestation and day-to-day functioning. I will propose a better naming scheme for these two.

2 Spectrums: We imagine a Venn Diagram, 1 of Quirks, and 1 of Disabling Features. Each category has a spectrum, say from 0-100. A person can have a high or low score in each of them, but they are not one spectrum for the Love of God. This ideology comes from a hyper wish to cluster up people into large groups; that's a trend in the world.

Quirks

Aka "High Functioning" aspects. Quirks entitle that there is something different about you, not good, not wrong, but different. These differences bring forth benefits and downsides.
What Are They? These traits will make one "a little different." Different preferences, actions, interests, and communication choices.
Downsides: You must be aware of the downsides and consciously work on keeping up with the rest of the world in those areas. These "high functioning traits," or Quirks, have the disadvantage of a low innate understanding of human beings. This manifests the most "live" in a conversation. After the conversation, we could be very clear about what happened there, especially if we have systems like the ones presented in this book "tattooed" in our brains. Innate refers to automatic understanding, which isn't sufficient for this kind of people, so systems of knowledge have to be added.
Benefits: Regarding the benefits, you need to double down on them, hell, even triple down. You will go to extremes that most people won't go to. You will find and see things that others cannot. You need to follow your intuition and your vision, for you cannot copy others (generally speaking). That extreme interest in things will eventually mature into something beautiful and appreciated by the world, or at least part of the world.
Attitude: Regarding "High-Functioning" autism, you can use jokes or be harsher to the people who have it and are complaining about it. "Stop complaining, get good at something," or jokingly, "Weaponize your autism." Motivation with comical relief, for you are not disabled. You are different, and you need to put that difference to good use, and you will be satisfied with your life.

Disabling Functions

Aka "Low Functioning". They are disabling because they genuinely turn off parts of your life. When such mechanisms are triggered, you cannot function properly.

What Are They? If you score on the spectrum and read about autism manifestations, you can look up the traits and manifestations of autism. You'll find general lists; you won't find them presented here as two separate items. Look at those traits that interrupt functioning in the world in a meaningful enough way.

Acceptance: There is no benefit to these, there isn't. You don't draw pros and cons from something life-disrupting. It is what it is. You learn to work around them as well as you can.

Attitude: Regarding "Low-Functioning" autism, your inner monologue or dialogue should be more empathic, softer, warmer, and loving. You don't need a slap on the back and a motivational speech when you have an inner situation that disrupts your life and functioning.

From The Outside: When confronted with disabling features, you deal with that with attention, understanding, and care. In high school, I've had the opportunity to work with kids with various disabilities, mental or physical. The difference between what I saw there and what you read online about life disrupting inner situations and a "Quirk" is immense.

Psychiatry 101

Psychiatry vs. Psychology

The easiest way to define and contemplate the two is by understanding what they are adjacent to.

Psychology: This is closer to philosophy. It concerns how you think, reason, view yourself, and understand the world.
Psychiatry: This is closer to medical care. These are situations where the way you think can't fix your problem. A psychiatrist must be able to read people and have understanding and training in reading people regarding psychological situations. But at the end of the day, medication as a solution to an illness is at the core here. Without proper medication, symptoms will always come back in mental illnesses.

General Overview Of Psychiatric Terms

We will offer a baseline of understanding here. So that you can spot if any of these things happen to the people around you or in society or if you have a clue that they are happening to you.

Schizophrenia

Schizophrenia is a lifelong diagnosis. Which, unfortunately, can cause early dementia. An early name for schizophrenia was 'dementia praecox' if you ever stumble upon this term.

Paranoid:
- **'Positive' Symptoms:** Hallucinations, delusions.
- **'Negative' Symptoms:** Also symptoms (negative) include apathy, extreme social withdrawal (imperative hallucinations make them isolate themselves), anhedonia, hypobulia (lack of action), flat or inappropriate affect
- **Disorganized:** Disorganized behavior, disorganized speech, random roll of words.

Disorganized: Disorganized behavior, disorganized speech, random roll of words.
Residual:
- **'Positive' Symptoms:** Exaggerated odd beliefs, unusual physical sensations (inner bodily hallucinations).
- **'Negative' Symptoms:** Blunted affect. [social withdrawal]

Catatonic:
- **'Positive' Symptoms:** Excited catatonia (perpetual exaggerated movements), stereotyped movements (repetitive, for example, back and forth rocking), echolalia (repeats what is said to them), echopraxia (imitates precisely what others do).
- **'Negative' Symptoms:** Catalepsy (muscular rigidity), waxy flexibility (stuck in weird positions), mutism.

Undifferentiated: Meets the criteria for multiple versions of schizophrenia.
Cenesthopathic:
- **'Positive' Symptoms:** unusual physical sensations (inner bodily hallucinations)

Psychotic Episode: A Singular manifestation of one of the types of schizophrenia.

Bipolar Disorder

It is characterized first by at least one manic or hypomanic (lighter manic episode) episode. The "bi" in bipolar stands for having both these kinds of "high" stakes and "low" states, which are depressive episodes.

Note that these episodes last quite a while and are not daily occurrences.

Mania:
- **Positively Perceived Symptoms:** Extreme joy, a connection to the Divine, reckless spending, hypersexuality, indestructibility, megalomania, high extraversion (positive emotion), expansive, increased talking speed.
- **Negatively Perceived Symptoms:** Extreme irascibility, racing thoughts, problems concentrating, pressure of speech (feels obligated to express verbally), risky behavior.
- **Duration:** Minimum a week to months.
- **Hypomania:** Is less intense and tends to last a shorter period. Another way to think about it is that with mania, most likely, you have to be brought to a psych ward. The states are so intense that you cannot understand what is going on with you. In a hypomanic state, you can still more or less function and be treated ambulatory. Note that both of these examples are without the person being on appropriate medication.
- **Type:** We see a person that had a manic episode as Type 1 bipolar and Type 2 where the episodes keep themselves in a hypomanic state and don't go higher.

Mixed: These episodes contain elements from both mania and depression. This state is easily confounded with borderline personality disorder.

Depression:
- **Symptoms:** Low tone of voice, heavy body, anhedonia (lack of happiness from the things previously brought you happiness), decreased libido, rumination, hopelessness, nihilism, fatalism, suicidal thoughts, suicide planning, suicide attempts.
- **Duration:** Last for a minimum of two weeks to months.
- **Bipolar:** Without medical treatment, it tends to escalate to a major depressive episode. Also, by the nature of bipolarity, it comes before a manic episode and especially after one.
- **Psychological:** This is not at a psychiatric level. This is your run-of-the-mill depression that a lot of people experience throughout their lives. That is one of the reasons that psychiatric depression is hard to comprehend for most because it is the same type of sensation but manifested at a completely different magnitude.
- **Unipolar:** Depression in the absence of manic episodes. It lasts less than a bipolar episode. It is at a psychiatric level and can range anywhere from anywhere from a mild episode to a major one.

Schizo-Affective Disorder: A combination between schizophrenia and bipolar disorder. Manic/depressive episodes + positive symptoms from schizophrenia.

Cyclothymia: We could call it a psychological level of bipolarity, where medication is not needed. The described states are similar but do not intervene negatively enough in the person's life. You can successfully live with it without a prescription.

Personal Experience & Observations: Note that people with bipolar disorder usually experience milder episodes at first, which are hard to notice from the outside. These episodes can escalate in time. Having this information, you have the essential tools to observe if you have periods like this in your life and be aware of what they could mean.

Dementia

Alzheimer's is characterized by forgetfulness.
- **Initial:** This forgetfulness debuts by forgetting recent events.
- **Mid:** As the illness progresses, the patient starts forgetting elements that happened some years ago. Their memory is partial, and the mind adds fragments to their memories that didn't occur.
- **Later Stages:** In the later stages, they forget their beginnings in this life, which leads to forgetting who the people in their lives are. The forgetfulness brings with it disorientation in terms of chronology (what time or even year it is) and spatial recognition (they don't know where they are).
- **End Stages:** At the end stages, they forget how to dress, speak, and eventually eat.

Other Types Are treated in the field of neurology. Other types include vascular dementia (caused by strokes), Lewy body dementia (accumulation of Lewy bodies-proteins in the brain), Parkinson-induced dementia, alcohol-related brain injury, and HIV-associated dementia (in the later stage of the disease when HIV infection becomes AIDS).

Anxiety Disorders

These are not your personality traits and natural tendencies. These disorders are exacerbated issues that may benefit from medication, not just therapy alone. Medication plays a role in treating these disorders if therapy doesn't work alone.

Panic Disorder: Characterized by panic attacks. A panic attack is when you feel extreme fear and thoughts of losing your mind or fainting/dying. It might also be confused with a heart attack. You can also experience massive fear over another possible future panic attack, which we call anticipatory anxiety.

Generalized Anxiety Disorder: Characterized by extreme worries about each aspect of a person's life. They might also be accompanied by muscle tension, insomnia, trouble thinking, and difficulty concentrating.

Health Anxiety Disorder: Also known as hypochondria. Extreme fear of getting ill in the future. For example, a person can have a random pain in their body and then jump instantly to the conclusion that it might be cancer and they are going to die soon. Driven by this fear, they tend to get many medical tests to ensure nothing is going on; even if the doctors tell them they are healthy, they don't buy it.

Social Anxiety: Extreme fear of talking in public or in front of a group of people, even if they are your friends.

Obsessive Compulsive Disorder: OCD is characterized by obsessive thoughts and compulsions. The person who suffers from OCD believes that these compulsions have the power to stop the obsessive thoughts from happening. For example, a person might think that if they unlock and lock their door 3 times in a row, they protect a loved one from dying.

Post Traumatic Stress Disorder: PTSD, characterized by flashbacks, nightmares, and extreme fear that something that has happened in the past might happen again.

Medication & A Better Lifestyle

People are reticent towards taking psychiatric medication. First, it is the social stigma. People tend to group people in too specific categories. So, by taking medication for these issues, they subconsciously identify it with some film about an asylum or with people yelling on the streets. That is not the case; these issues have a broad spectrum of intensities. What you see on the roads are people higher on the spectrum of intensity for these illnesses and also are not on medication.

Know That: Also, there is a general pattern of people ceasing their medication after they are cured of their first episode. It doesn't just 'go away' if you are rightfully and correctly diagnosed. By ceasing it, you open yourself up to a severe next episode. If you were on medication, that episode would have been manageable and uninterrupted in your life. This is an ordinary urge that happens in many, if not most, people. If you have an urge like that, know you are not alone. Also, know the fact that the initial part of taking medication has more mental side effects than what you will experience in the future. You will have to wait it out for a while till things settle down.

www.ingramcontent.com/pod-product-compliance
Lightning Source LLC
Chambersburg PA
CBHW041042120726
48006CB00017B/2315